Schriften der Ernst von Caemmerer-Stiftung

Band 8

Prof. Dr. Uwe Blaurock (ed.)

The Influence of Islam
on Banking and Finance

Nomos

Die Deutsche Nationalbibliothek lists this publication in the
Deutsche Nationalbibliografie; detailed bibliographic data
is available in the Internet at http://dnb.d-nb.de

ISBN   978-3-8487-1824-5 (Print)
        978-3-8452-5822-5 (ePDF)

British Library Cataloguing-in-Publication Data
A catalogue record for this book is available from the British Library.

ISBN   978-3-8487-1824-5 (Print)
        978-3-8452-5822-5 (ePDF)

Library of Congress Cataloging-in-Publication Data
Blaurock, Uwe
The Influence of Islam on Banking and Finance
Prof. Dr. Uwe Blaurock (ed.)
76 p.

ISBN   978-3-8487-1824-5 (Print)
        978-3-8452-5822-5 (ePDF)

1. Edition 2014
© Nomos Verlagsgesellschaft, Baden-Baden, Germany 2014. Printed and bound in Germany.

Preface

On the 12th of October 2012, the Ernst von Caemmerer Foundation organized a colloquium on "The Influence of Islam on Finance and Banking" that took place in the premises of the Commerzbank AG in Frankfurt am Main. Subject of the presentations and subsequent discussions were the latest developments in the field of Islamic Banking and its position in the international financial system.

The present anthology contains the presentations held at the Colloquium as well as the respective discussion reports. The written versions of the presentations by Dr. Mehmet Asutay on "The Influence of Islamic Principles on Banking and Finance" and by habib Motani on "Islamic Finance" were unfortunately not available A summary of their content ist provided as replacement.

For the complete conference report see *Elias Bischof*, The Influence of Islam on Banking and Finance: A Conference Report, 2013, 24 I.C.C.L.R. – International Company and Commercial Law Review, 369 – 374.

Freiburg im Breisgau, May 2014   Uwe Blaurock

Table of Contents

Opening remarks

Uwe Blaurock[*]

On behalf of the Ernst von Caemmerer Foundation I cordially welcome you to this colloquium "The Influence of Islam on Banking and Finance". While this topic has been discussed in Frankfurt on several occasions, it has recently become particularly relevant. These days, here in Frankfurt an Islamic bank is going to be established. It is a Turkish bank, which will work according to the rules of the Sharia.

First of all I would like to thank the Commerzbank for their valuable contributions and for providing their rooms. Without the assistance of the Commerzbank it would not have been possible for the Foundation to organize this colloquium in Frankfurt.

Let me start with a few words about the Ernst von Caemmerer Foundation:

The Foundation was established 25 years ago by the postdoctoral research fellows of Ernst von Caemmerer, a former Law professor at the University of Freiburg. Its purpose is the promotion of science and research in the field of law and in particular in the fields of private law and comparative law, which were investigated by the foundation's eponym, Ernst von Caemmerer, whose memory shall be preserved.

This occurs in two different ways: First, the foundation awards scholarships to foreign lawyers for free research visits in Germany. The awarding of these scholarships is linked to the condition that the scholars prepare a scientific publication in the areas covered by the foundation's purpose during their stay in Germany. The second field of activity of the Foundation is the organization of academic colloquia. In the past several colloquia discussing mainly topics of the law of obligations from a comparative legal perspective have taken place. The respective lectures were subse-

---

[*] Professor of Law, Institute of Commercial Law, University of Freiburg/Germany; Chairman of the Ernst von Caemmerer Foundation.

quently published in the publication series of the Foundation as edited volumes.

The arising legal issues concerning the applicability of religious rules on obligations have previously been addressed by the Ernst von Caemmerer Foundation. For example, in 2004 an Egyptian scholar, Mr. Sherif El Saadani, studied the obligation to pay interest according to Art. 78 and Art. 84 (1) CISG during his research visit in Freiburg and published an extensive article on "The Islamic prohibition of interest and sale contracts under the CISG-"[1] In light of the recent significant changes in the Arabic world as well as the increasing importance of predominantly Muslim countries in international banking, the foundation decided to put a focus on this topic by organizing a colloquium with the purpose of examining the influence of Islam on banking and finance. We are fortunate to have the Commerzbank AG as our cooperation partner, which on the one hand is closely associated with the Foundation and on the other hand perfectly suited to provide a framework for a fruitful discussion given their international connections and practical experience.

Islamic banking is understood as banking according to Islamic principles.[2] In general it includes all types of financial services that can be handled in accordance with the Sharia, even if they are subordinated to a secular jurisdiction.[3] During the past one hundred years a modern banking system developed in the Islamic world, with the majority of banks operating conventionally and interest-based[4]. Each country's civil and commercial law that applies to these transactions is principally based on European role models.[5] However, the market for financial products designed according to specific Islamic rules is growing significantly. At the World Islamic Funds Conference of 2009 in Bahrain, the auditing company Ernst & Young expected that the market would pass the limit of one trillion dollars in 2010. The annual growth rate of the global market was estimated to be

---

1   *Sherif El Saadani*, Freilaw – Freiburg Law Students Journal III – 10/2006, p. 1 – 52.

2   *Bälz*, ZVglRWiss 109 (2010), p. 272 (275) with further references.

3   *Heckel*, ZVglRWiss 111 (2012), 311 (312).

4   For more details see *Azzam*, The Emerging Arab Capital Markets, 1997; *Henry*, The Mediterian Debt Crescent, 1996.

5   *Bälz*, loc. cit.

20%.[6] At the Islamic Funds Conference in May 2012, it was emphasized that just the volume of Islamic bonds – which are referred to as "Sukuk" – had more than doubled compared to the pre-crisis period (2007), while this increase could be primarily attributed to the development in Malaysia.

Compared to the volume of the entire conventional debt market, trading with Islamic financial products is still a niche market despite their growth. However, this market is not limited to banks or customers from Islamic countries. Most of the big Western banks opened "windows to the Islamic World"[7] and one of the largest European banks, the BNP-Paribas, recently reported that more than 20% of the investors in a Sukuk offered by them came from European countries[8]. By now there is a Dow-Jones index for the Islamic market, which registers hundreds of companies (not only from Islamic countries), that comply with the provisions of the Sharia.[9]

So, what are these "Islamic principles" anyways? Of importance to the banking sector are

- the general prohibition of interest (Riba)
- the prohibition of speculation (Gharar)
- the prohibition of gambling (Maysir).

These principles primarily affect all kinds of financing transactions, futures, securitizations of risk, short-term trade in securities as well as plain insurance business.

For instance, an Islamic bank has to participate in both profits and losses of its customers instead of paying a fixed interest rate. Also, for equity transactions, crisis expediting instruments such as derivatives and short sales are just as off-limits as transactions with companies who bring too little equity.[10]

---

6 Handelsblatt v. 4.6.2009.
7 http://www.monde-diplomatique.de/pm/2001/09/14/a0019.text.name,ask
   7LDPjA.n,16.
8 http://www.bloomberg.com/news/print/2012-06-05/bnp-paribas-alwi-says-more-
   non-islamic-investors-buying-sukuk.html.
9 http://www.monde-diplomatique.de/pm/2001/09/14/a0019.text.name,ask
   7LDPjA.n,16.
10 FAZ v. 2.5.2012, p. 4.

In addition, there are ethical exclusion criteria to be complied with that prohibit investments in

- alcohol production or trading
- prostitution
- pornography
- the processing of pork or trading products which contain pork

This particularly concerns the composition of funds and the financing of companies in these sectors. Clearly, the compliance with these ethical rules is often subject to uncertainty. For example it may be difficult to determine whether movies produced by a company that a fund invests in include pornographic content.

These uncertainties are further increased by the fact that there is no complete agreement on the exact content of the "Islamic principles". Therefore, legal opinions (Fatwa) are of considerable importance and play a central role in Islamic banking. Banks which offer products complying with the Sharia usually have a Sharia Board consisting of legal experts for that reason. They advise the bank and continuously assure that the said products remain in accordance with the Sharia. The seal of approval issued by this board is worded in a similar way as an auditor's certificate.[11] During today's colloquium, we are thus dealing with an area in which (apart from the laws of Iran, Saudi Arabia and Sudan) special problems arise due to the coexistence of state law and religious rules. Certainly, one could locate the Islamic banking close to the field of Social Responsible Investment, which is to regard it as a form of global business ethics.[12] To me at least this point of view appears too simplistic. The Sharia is not merely an extra-legal system of obligations but a legal order by itself. Even after complementation and interference by state rules it still has a far-reaching significance, being the former common law of the Islamic world.[13]

Today, the morning session is headed by Mr. Najam Ahmed Khan and initially dedicated to provide fundamental information. In this context Dr.

---

11 For more details see *Bälz*, ZVglRWiss 109 (2010), p. 272 (278)
12 See *Bälz*, ibid., p. 291 f.
13 See *Johannsen*, Contingency in a Sacred Law, 1999, p. 43 ff.

Mehmet Asutay of the University of Durham is going to lecture about the general theme "The Influence of Islamic Principles on Banking and Finance". In the following, Dr. Thomas Prüm addresses the more specific topic "Islamic Capital Markets".

In the first afternoon session chaired by Professor Dr. Martin Schmidt-Kessel, Mr. Habib Motani is going to discuss the different Sharia conform financing options in his report about "Islamic Finance". The second afternoon session under the chairmanship of Professor Dr. Peter Jung then shifts the focus to the non-Islamic world. Professor Dr. Matthias Casper of the University of Münster is going to draw comparisons to European rules in his lecture "Sharia Boards and Sharia compliance in the context of European governance". Finally, Professor Dr. Dr. h.c. Herbert Kronke of the University of Heidelberg is going to address the fundamental question of our current state in the globalization of bank contract law in the closing report "Towards a Global Contract Law in Banking and Finance? Inventory and Perspectives".

I am looking forward to the reports and I am hoping that we will have interesting discussions during our colloquium.

Islamic Moral Economy Foundations of Islamic Finance

Mehmet Asutay[*]

Content and Discussion report to the lecture of Mehmet Asutay

Elias Bischof[**]

I. Content

Dr. *Asutay* ascribes the origin of Islamic Banking and Finance (IBF) to the development of an Islamic moral economy in the post-colonial and post-World War II period. The IBF can be seen to be a human-centric answer derived from the sources of Islam (i.e. the Shari'a) whereas in the capitalist economy both the human being and his or her well-being are ignored.

Dr. *Asutay* states that the axioms of the Islamic moral economy to realise "human well-being" contain vertical (in relation to God) and horizontal (between individuals) equality, growth in harmony with stakeholders, striving for perfection and mandatory financial and economic obligations (*fard*). He explains that the implications of these fundamental assumptions affect every member of the society, including the needy. Society should firstly maximise its utility to maximise social welfare and secondly enable equal access to environmental and public resources. Property rights for instance are subject to moral limits and can be used as a means of fulfilling ethical objectives. Dr. *Asutay* states that market mechanism is seen as a fundamental pillar of the Islamic moral economy. The consequences of the market system have to be moderated by moral filters, e.g. by prohibiting

---

[*]   Director Islamic Finance, University of Durham.
[**]   lic.iur., LL.M. (Edinburgh); Rechtsanwalt and Mediator, bischoflaw, Basel; research assistant and doctoral candidate, University of Basel.

certain sources of income (interest, speculation, gambling), investment sectors (e.g. alcohol, armaments, financial services, gambling, pork, pornography, tobacco) and investment instruments (e.g. forward transactions, derivatives, short-selling). This system aims to ensure economic development and social justice in the society and also to satisfy the spiritual needs of all the members of the community. *Dr. Asutay* describes IBF as community banking, which promotes the investment mindset (investing in real assets) rather than the banking mindset (speculation and leverage).

Dr. Asutay continues to explain that these principles have led to Islamic regions being rather under-served and having un-banked markets until the 1960s, when an initial discovery of the IBF took place in Egypt and Malaysia. It was the oil-boom in the Gulf region in the early 1970s, which promoted the development of IBF as a novel, alternative method of finance. *Dr. Asutay* regrets that the IBF has increasingly converged towards conventional finance and its products since the 1990s, e.g. the increasing use of debt financing as opposed to profit-and-loss sharing (PLS) instruments, the search for Islamic derivatives, and short-term financing. This commercialisation and 'financialisation' (i.e. creating money and wealth from non-existing financial resources) of the IBF make Islamic finance more susceptible to consequences similar to the recent global financial crisis in 2008. *Dr. Asutay* advocates the preservation of IBF principles in the belief that the holistic approach of Islamic banking has the potential to enable economic developments.

II. Discussion

Prof. Dr. Carola Stumpf (Halle) states that the fundamental principles of the IBF such as the prohibition of gambling and interest, vertical and horizontal growth in harmony, responsibility of individuals etc. have been part of the legal tradition in Central Europe for a very long time, namely in the Canon Law, having been removed however bit by bit. Since 1822 the provisions prohibiting the levying of interest have gradually been relaxed and by 1983 were no longer mentioned in the *Codex Juris Canonici*.[1] For *Prof. Dr. Stumpf* one of the reasons for this convergence in Central Europe might have been the increased complexity in the allocation of goods.

Prof. Dr. Peter Jung (Basel) questions if the Shari'a requires banks, which do not exclusively deal with Shari'a compliant products, to establish separate business entities if they wish to engage in the IBF. – *Dr. Asutay* negates. It is not the institution which is problematic, but the financial product itself. *Dr. Asutay* however concedes that a substantial number of Islamic scholars do however lack the necessary economic knowledge. It is difficult for them to see the wider economic implications in the specific case of a financial institution.

---

1   The prohibition of interest on interest is still contained to a certain extent in several civil law jurisdictions, see e.g. § 248(1) of the German BGB or Art 105(3) of the Swiss Code of Obligations.

Islamic Capital Markets

*Thomas Prüm**

I. Introduction

This paper is based on a presentation made at the conference of the foundation *"Ernst von Caemmerer-Gedächtnisstiftung"* held in Frankfurt/Main on 12 October 2012. It discusses selected German law aspects of financial products traded in the Islamic Capital Markets from a German viewpoint. Islamic Capital Markets can be understood as capital markets in which all transactions are carried out in a way that does not conflict with the religion and the principles of the Islam.[1]

The normative principles of the Islam are derived from the Sharia, which governs both interpersonal relationships as well as the relationship between the individual and God.[2] The key principles of the Sharia in turn are derived from the Quran as well as the Sunna[3] which itself is derived from acts and speeches (*Hadit*) of the prophet Mohammed.[4]

Common financial products that are Sharia conform[5] include funds[6], shares in corporations which conform to the Sharia[7] and Sharia compliant

---

*   Partner, Berwin Leighton Paisner, Frankfurt a.M.
1   *Gassner/Wackerbeck*, Islamic Finance, 2d edition, Köln 2010, p. 21, 52; *Grieser*, WM 2009, 586; see also *Ayub*, Understanding Islamic Finance, Chichester 2008, p. 43 et seq and p. 390 et seq.; *El-Gamal*, Islamic Finance, Law, Economics and Practice, New York 2006, p. 107.
2   *Wiedensohler*, RabelsZ 35, 632, 633; *Sacarcelik*, Rechtsfragen islamischer Zertifikate (Sukuk), Baden-Baden 2013, p. 33; *Gassner/Wackerbeck*, Islamic Finance, p. 32; *Yassari*, ZfRV 1999, 103, 104; *Bälz*, ZVglRWiss 109 (2010), 272.
3   *Schacht*, An Introduction to Islamic Law, Oxford 1964, p. 112; *Trinkaus/Prüm*, CORPORATE FINANCE law 2010, 147.
4   *Yassari*, ZfRV 1999, 103, 104.
5   See also *Trinkaus/Prüm*, CORPORATE FINANCE law 2010, 147.
6   *Caspar*, Islamische Aktienfonds – eine kapitalmarktrechtliche Herausforderung?, Festschrift für Uwe H. Schneider, 2011, 229, 231; *Bälz*, BKR 2002, 447; *Gassner/Wackerbeck*, Islamic Finance, p. 170.

capital market instruments. Capital market instruments that are especially designed to conform to the Sharia include in particular Sukuks.[8] "Sukuk" is the Arabic term for certificates but usually refers to the Islamic equivalent for bonds.[9] Over the last two decades Sukuk have become an increasingly popular instrument for the financing of Islamic undertakings and projects.[10]

The popularity of Sukuk had suffered slightly after the beginning of the financial crises in 2007; in particular Sukuk spread widened after the financial crisis when the asset bubble bursts in the Arab region.[11] In the last years the demand for Sukuk and the limited supply resulted in a tightening relative to conventional counterparts. There has been a clear increase in activity over the last months.[12]

Although the issuance of Sukuk is clearly focussed on the Arabic and Asian parts of the world rather than Europe there have been a few examples of Sukuk in Europe.[13] The first European Sukuk (in the nominal amount of EUR 100 million) has been issued by the state of Saxony-Anhalt in Germany in the year 2004.[14] The Sukuk was based on an *Ijarah* (sale and leaseback) structure[15] and was backed by properties of the state of Saxony-Anhalt.[16] Enhanced by a guarantee of the state, this Sukuk was a sovereign risk instrument.[17] In 2009, it was repaid. When the state of Saxony-Anhalt entered into the transaction, it intended to build a bridge

---

7   An instructive example for this form of investment gives BGH, ruling of 29.11.2011 – VI ZR 251/10 (OLG Düsseldorf), BeckRS 2011, 27601; see *Brocker*, GWR 2012, 41.

8   *Ayub*, Understanding Islamic Finance, p. 390; *Gassner/Wackerbeck*, Islamic Finance, p.122; *Sacarcelik*, Rechtsfragen islamischer Zertifikate (Sukuk), p. 45.

9   *Sacarcelik*, Rechtsfragen islamischer Zertifikate (Sukuk), p. 54.

10 *Müller*, WM 2008, 102; *Gassner/Wackerbeck*, Islamic Finance, p. 122.

11 *Sacarcelik*, Rechtsfragen islamischer Zertifikate (Sukuk), p. 49.

12 http://gulfnews.com/business/banking/global-sukuk-issuance-poised-for-a-big-leap-1.1261790.

13 With respect to the potential in corporate finance see *Trinkaus/Prüm*, CORPORATE FINANCE law 2010, 147 et seq.

14 *Stichting Sachsen-Anhalt Trust*; *Gassner/Wackerbeck*, Islamic Finance, p. 133.

15 See prospectus for the *Stichting Sachsen-Anhalt Trust*, p. 9.

16 See prospectus for the *Stichting Sachsen-Anhalt Trust*, p. 9 and the definition of „Trust Assets".

17 *Gassner/Wackerbeck*, Islamic Finance, p. 134.

into the Islamic (in particular Arabic) world and to market the industry in Saxony-Anhalt to Islamic investors.[18]

Following the first European Sukuk in Germany there have been various efforts to issue other European Sukuks including sovereign Sukuk; in particular the United Kingdom, France and Luxembourg have worked on several Sukuk. With respect to corporate Sukuks it was again Germany[19] which saw the first corporate Sukuk of a visible size (USD 55 million): In 2012, a German corporate based in Munich entered into a Sukuk transaction.[20] Most recently, the United Kingdom announced that it will soon issue a Sukuk.[21] However, so far there has been only one small ticket transaction in the United Kingdom.[22] Also in Turkey it took almost 8 years until a first sovereign Sukuk was placed.[23] However, also in Turkey the popularity of the instrument Sukuk seems to be increasing.[24]

Sukuk are the predominant product in the Islamic capital market space.[25] For this reason this article focuses on Sukuk. From a western law perspective, the main risk which is different from the risk in a conventional bond structure is the so-called "Sharia Risk".[26] The Sharia Risk stems from the fact that there is no central Islamic authority in Sharia matters. This results in the risk that one authority takes a different view than another authority with respect to the Sharia compliance of a Sukuk. As discussed below in more detail this Sharia Risk materialised in 2008 with the ruling of Sheik Taqi Usmani who took the view that a substantial amount of Sukuk did not conform to the Sharia.[27] Since 2008 the industry, in particular through the *Accounting and Auditing Organization for Islamic Fi-*

---

18   *Gassner/Wackerbeck*, Islamic Finance, p. 134.
19   The history of modern Islamic Banking also started in Germany; see *Gassner/Wackerbeck*, Islamic Finance, p. 50.
20   http://www.zawya.com/story/USD55m_FWU_sukuk_sets_new_standards-ZAWYA20130111143827.
21   http://uk.reuters.com/article/2013/10/29/uk-britain-finance-islamic-idUKBRE99S00I20131029.
22   *Sacarcelik*, Rechtsfragen islamischer Zertifikate (Sukuk), p. 47.
23   *Sacarcelik*, Rechtsfragen islamischer Zertifikate (Sukuk), p. 48.
24   *Sacarcelik*, Rechtsfragen islamischer Zertifikate (Sukuk), p. 48.
25   *Trinkaus/Prüm*, CORPORATE FINANCE law 2010, 147, 151; *Ayub*, Understanding Islamic Finance, p. 390.
26   *Caspar*, CORPORATE FINANCE law 2012, 170, 172.
27   *Bälz*, ZVglRWiss 109 (2010), 272, 292.

nancial Institutions (AAOIFI)[28] has made substantial efforts to create a reliable basis for Sukuk issuances.[29]

II. Sukuk structures

AAOIFI has defined Sukuk as follows: „Sukuk are certificates of equal value representing undivided shares in ownership of tangible assets, usufruct and services or (in the ownership of) the assets of particular projects or special investment activity, however, this is true after the receipt of the value of the Sukuk, the closing of the subscription and employment of funds received for the purpose for which the Sukuk were issued."[30]

The Securities Commission of Malaysia has a similar definition of Sukuk: „Certificates of equal value which evidence undivided ownership or interest in the assets using Sharia principles and concepts endorsed by Sharia Advisory Council.[31]

These and other definitions have in common that Sukuk are certificates of equal value that represent ownership in some kind of investment.[32] Although a Sukuk can be structured in various forms[33], Sukuk typically have some basic structural elements in common[34]: In general a Sukuk is issued by a special purpose vehicle (SPV) which has been established by the originator. The Sukuk is issued in exchange for cash. The SPV purchases assets from the originator using the proceeds of the Sukuk issuance that was held in trust for the investors. The assets the SPV has purchased from the originator generate revenues that are used to return a profit to the investors corresponding to their ownership interest.

---

28 http://www.aaoifi.com.
29 *Trinkaus/Prüm*, CORPORATE FINANCE law 2010, 147, 151.
30 AAOIFI FAS 25 - Investment in Sukuk, Shares and Similar Instruments.
31 Suruhanjaya Sekuriti – Securities Commission Malaysia, Guidelines on Sukuk, effective 8 January 2014.
32 *Ayub*, Understanding Islamic Finance, p. 389 et seq.
33 *Müller*, WM 2008, 102, 103; *Sacarcelik*, Rechtsfragen islamischer Zertifikate (Sukuk), p. 57 et seq.; *Gassner/Wackerbeck*, Islamic Finance, p. 127 et seq.
34 *Sacarcelik*, Rechtsfragen islamischer Zertifikate (Sukuk), p. 57 et seq.; *Gassner/Wackerbeck*, Islamic Finance, p. 127 et seq.; *Müller*, WM 2008, 102, 104; *Trinkaus/Prüm*, CORPORATE FINANCE law 2010, 147, 151.

1. Sukuk al Ijarah

A *Sukuk al Ijarah* is structured as follows[35]: An *Ijahra* is a usufruct type of contract based on the Adq (contract); a lessor (owner) leases out an asset or equipment to the lessee at an agreed rental fee and pre-determined lease period, through sale and leaseback arrangement.[36] The lessee makes periodic rental payments which correspond to the periodic distributions under the Sukuk. The investors in the Sukuk al Ijarah are entitled to undivided beneficial ownership of the asset or equipment.

2. Sukuk al Musharakah

A *Sukuk al Musharakah* is structured as follows[37]: A *Musharakah* is a joint venture in which partners share the profit and loss of an enterprise. The partners make a certain contribution.[38] The SPV is entitled to the assets of the partnership and the profit, whereby the profit will be distributed to the investors at an agreed upon ratio.

3. Sukuk al Istisna'a

In a typical *Sukuk al Istisna'a*[39] the originator enters into an agreement with the SPV, whereby the originator agrees to manufacture or construct an asset for delivery to the SPV at a later date.[40] The SPV, in turn, agrees

---

35 *Trinkaus/Prüm*, CORPORATE FINANCE law 2010, 147, 151; *Sacarcelik*, Rechtsfragen islamischer Zertifikate (Sukuk), p. 177 et seq.; *Gassner/Wackerbeck*, Islamic Finance, p. 128 et seq.
36 *Kettell*, Introduction to Islamic banking and finance, Chichester 2011, p. 89 et seq.; *Ayub*, Understanding Islamic Finance, p. 279 et seq.
37 *Sacarcelik*, Rechtsfragen islamischer Zertifikate (Sukuk), p. 237 et seq.; *Gassner/Wackerbeck*, Islamic Finance, p. 130 et seq.; *Müller*, WM 2008, 102, 105; *Trinkaus/Prüm*, CORPORATE FINANCE law 2010, 147, 152.
38 *Kettell*, Introduction to Islamic banking and finance, p. 77 et seq.; *Ayub*, Understanding Islamic Finance, p. 312 et seq.
39 *Sacarcelik*, Rechtsfragen islamischer Zertifikate (Sukuk), p. 210 et seq.; *Gassner/Wackerbeck*, Islamic Finance, p. 144 et seq.
40 *Kettell*, Introduction to Islamic banking and finance, p. 103 et seq.

to pay the construction or manufacturing cost of the asset in instalments as certain milestones are achieved. The SPV issues the Sukuk certificates and receives the purchase price for these certificates in order to pay the price for the manufacture and construction of the assets. The SPV owns the asset in trust for the Sukuk holders. Each Sukuk holder has an undivided ownership interest in the asset proportionate to the value of their investment. Each Sukuk holder is entitled to receive a return on their investment in proportion to the amount of their Sukuk interests. Once the asset has been constructed, title to the asset is transferred to the SPV. The SPV leases the assets to the originator. The originator makes rental payments (advance payments and actual rental payments). The SPV, in turn, uses the rental payments to pay periodic distribution amounts to the Sukuk holders under the Sukuk. The SPV and the originator enter into a purchase undertaking which gives the SPV the right to sell the constructed assets to the originator at maturity of the Sukuk or if a default has occurred. If the SPV sells the asset back to the originator, the SPV uses the proceeds of the asset sales to redeem the Sukuk certificates. If the SPV had not taken delivery of the asset at the time of the default or, at maturity, the SPV had not yet taken delivery of the asset, instead of selling the asset to the originator, the SPV has the right to receive a refund of any amounts it has paid to the originator minus any advance rental amounts (the Istisna'a termination amount). In this case, the SPV must also refund any advance rental payments the originator may have paid to it. The originator and the SPV are also parties to a service agreement. The originator agrees to operate and maintain the assets on behalf of the SPV, including obtaining insurance and overseeing repairs. The service agreement is structured as follows: The originator is paid for any costs and expenses it incurs in connection with its management of the assets, rental payment is due after these costs are incurred and are increased by the amount of the costs and expenses, and the originator's obligations to pay rent on the assets is typically reduced by the amount of the costs and expenses. As a result of this structure, the assets are maintained, and the rent the SPV receives equals the amount the SPV would have received, if such costs had not been incurred. Historically (up to 2007), the purchase price for the assets or the *Istisna'a* termination amount was equal to the principal amount outstanding under the Sukuk plus any accrued and unpaid periodic distribution amounts.

4. Sukuk al Murabaha

In a typical *Sukuk al Murabaha*[41] the SPV issues the Sukuk. The SPV buys an asset from a third party.[42] The SPV immediately sells the asset to the originator/borrower for the original purchase price plus a profit element. The borrower pays the purchase price in instalments on a deferred basis. The SPV uses the amounts it receives to make periodic distribution amounts to the Sukuk holders. After the sales, the third party has received full and immediate payment for the asset, but the obligations of the borrower under the purchase agreement with the SPV are on a deferred basis. Unlike other Sukuk transactions, the Sukuk holders do not have a proportionate interest in the assets because those assets are subsequently sold to the borrower. Instead, the Sukuk holders have a proportionate interest in the SPV's receivables (the borrower's obligation to pay the purchase price to the SPV).

5. Sukuk al Mudaraba

In a typical *Sukuk al Mudaraba*[43] the party seeking financing (the *Mudareb*) enters into an agreement (the *Mudaraba* agreement[44]) with a SPV, pursuant to which it agrees to manage certain specified assets owned by the SPV. The SPV issues the Sukuk to investors. The SPV gives the proceeds of the Sukuk issuance to the *Mudareb* to invest in Sharia compliant investments which will be owned by the SPV on behalf of the Sukuk holders. In exchange for its management of the investments, the *Mudareb* receives a fee from any profits earned from the investments. The remainder of any profits are paid to the SPV which in turn uses these funds to make periodic distribution amounts to the Sukuk holders. The *Mudareb*

---

41 *Sacarcelik*, Rechtsfragen islamischer Zertifikate (Sukuk), p. 199 et seq.
42 For a more detailled discussion of the Murabaha structure see *Ayub*, Understanding Islamic Finance, p. 213 et seq.; *Trinkaus/Prüm*, CORPORATE FINANCE law 2010, 147, 150.
43 *Sacarcelik*, Rechtsfragen islamischer Zertifikate (Sukuk), p. 218 et seq.; *Müller*, WM 2008, 102, 104.
44 *Kettell*, Introduction to Islamic banking and finance, p. 63 et seq.; *Trinkaus/Prüm*, CORPORATE FINANCE law 2010, 152.

enters into a purchase undertaking with the SPV pursuant to which the SPV has the right to cause the originator to buy all or a portion of the Mudaraba assets. The price has to be determined in a way causing the Sukuk holders to bear risk of loss with respect to the assets. The SPV uses the proceeds of the sale to redeem the Sukuk certificates.

6. Sukuk al Salam

A typical *Sukuk al Salam*[45] is structured as follows: The originator enters into a sale and purchase agreement with an SPV.[46] The originator agrees to sell certain assets to the SPV on a deferred delivery basis. The SPV agrees to pay the purchase price in advance. In consideration for the advance payment, the SPV typically receives a discount on the purchase price. The SPV issues the Sukuk. The SPV owns the assets in trust for the Sukuk holders. Each Sukuk holder has an undivided ownership interest in the assets proportionate to the value of their investment. Each Sukuk holder is entitled to receive a return on their investment in proportion to the amount of their Sukuk interests. The SPV and the originator enter into another agreement under which the SPV either sells or leases the assets back to the originator. The rental payments or the purchase price are generally structured in a way which enables the Sukuk holders to receive their negotiated return on their Sukuk investment (the periodic distribution amounts). The purchase price or rental payments the originator pays exceed the amounts the SPV paid for the assets. The difference between the two amounts is how the SPV earns a profit on the transaction.

---

45 *Müller*, WM 2008, 102, 105; *Sacarcelik*, Rechtsfragen islamischer Zertifikate (Sukuk), p. 207 et seq.
46 *Kettell*, Introduction to Islamic banking and finance, p. 117 et seq.; *Ayub*, Understanding Islamic Finance, p. 241 et seq.

7. Sukuk al Wakala

A typical *Sukuk al Wakala* is structured as follows[47]: The SPV issues the Sukuk. The SPV uses the proceeds to make investments on behalf of the investors. The SPV enters into a *Wakala* (agency) agreement with the originator to invest the funds in Sharia compliant assets on behalf of the SPV. The SPV receives a specified amount from the profits earned from investing the *Wakala* assets. Profits generated in excess of the agreed amount are paid to the originator as an incentive fee. The SPV uses its share of the profits to pay periodic distribution amounts to the Sukuk holders under the Sukuk. To ensure the Sukuk holders are paid their required amounts, the SPV and the originator enter into a purchase undertaking pursuant to which the SPV has the right under certain circumstances to cause the originator to buy all or a portion of the *Wakala* assets. The *Sukuk al Wakala* has to be structured in a way that the Sukuk holders bear some risk of loss with respect to the assets.

III. Sharia conformity

According to an AAOIFI statement in 2007, in order to comply with the Sharia principles of shared risks and profit, the exercise price for the assets must be based on the market value of the assets at the time the originator exercises its rights under the purchase undertaking.[48] Many *Sukuk al Mudaraba* had a structure where the exercise price was equal to the amount of Sukuk issued. As a result, the Sukuk holders bore no risk of loss with respect to the assets and the instrument did not comply with the AAOIFI view. Following the intensive discussion among scholars and market participants, AAOIFI issued revised and clearer rules.[49]

---

47   *Ayub*, Understanding Islamic Finance, p. 347 et seq.
48   *Sacarcelik*, Rechtsfragen islamischer Zertifikate (Sukuk), p. 224; *Gassner/Wackerbeck*, Islamic Finance, p. 157.
49   http://www.aaoifi.com/en/content/search/?s=sukuk.

IV. Qualification of Sukuk under German Law

The legal classification of Sukuk is in particular of material importance for the treatment of this instrument under tax, regulatory and company law. For example, various obligations are imposed to an investment fund and if a Sukuk qualifies as a fund it would be subject to these rules. Since during the course of the Sukuk transaction assets are bundled in a pool and evidenced by document, the question is of relevance whether Sukuk may be categorized as investment fund according to the German Investment Act (*Investmentgesetz*; *InvG*) or its successor act, the German Investment Code (*Kapitalanlagengesetzbuch*; *KAGB*).[50] In particular with respect to property backed Sukuk transactions it needs to be clarified whether the classification as an investment fund is appropriate in individual cases. If Sukuk are categorized as funds within the meaning of the *InvG/KAGB*, numerous duties and special provisions under investment law would apply.

1. Classification under the InvG

Domestic Sukuks

Against the background of the replacement of the *InvG* by the German Investment Code (*KAGB*)[51] it should also be considered in a first step whether domestic or foreign Sukuk which are common in the respective market fall into the factual scope of the *InvG*. Pursuant to Sec. 7 Subsec. 1 of the *InvG* the funds business is subject to a permission requirement. Apart from the general requirements for such permit pursuant to Sec. 11 of the *InvG* there are in particular special requirements regarding the reliability and professional qualification of the managing directors (Sec. 7b, no. 3 of the *InvG*). Besides, corporations (*Kapitalgesellschaften*) are subject to a general code of conduct (Sec. 9 of the *InvG*), organizational duties (Sec. 10 of the *InvG*) and capital requirements (Sec. 11 of the *InvG*). In particu-

---

50 *Sacarcelik*, Rechtsfragen islamischer Zertifikate (Sukuk), p. 78 et seq.
51 Art. 2a Gesetz zur Umsetzung der Richtlinie 2011/61/EU über die Verwalter alternativer Investmentfonds.

lar the duty to publish a prospectus according to Sec. 42 of the *InvG* is of importance in that regard. Sukuks which are usually traded in the German market usually do not fulfil the requirements of domestic assets within the meaning of Sec. 2 Subsec. 1 of the *InvG*.

They do not fulfil the requirements of domestic assets (*inländisches Investmentvermögen*) because their structure does not correspond in form and substance to the structures which are subject to the regulation of the *InvG*.[52] Further, in general, there is no active management of the assets (*aktive Vermögensverwaltung*), on the basis of the principal of risk diversification (*Grundsatz der Risikomischung; Sec. 1 sentence 2 InvG*) and in accordance with predefined management principles (*vordefinierte Anlagegrundsätze; Sec. 43 Subsec. 4 no. 1 InvG*).

Foreign Sukuks

Foreign Sukuks which are offered publicly in Germany can be qualified as foreign investment units (*ausländische Investmentanteile*). According to the legal definition in Sec. 2 Subsec. 9 *InvG* foreign investment units qualify as units in foreign investment assets (*ausländische Investmentvermögen*) which have been sold by a company with corporate seat in another jurisdiction (*ausländische Investmentgesellschaft*) and if the unit holder can request that his portion in the foreign investment undertaking against return of his unit. Alternatively this would also apply if the unit holder has no right to return his unit, the foreign investment company, however, is subject to supervision and regulation in the jurisdiction of its corporate seat. As far as foreign Sukuks qualify as foreign investment units they are subject to the specific rules set out in the Secs. 136 ff. *InvG*. In particular they need to comply with the admission rules set out in Sec. 136 *InvG*. Further they are obliged in accordance with Sec. 139 *InvG* to notify the Federal Financial Supervisory Authority (*Bundesanstalt für Finanzdienstleistungsaufsicht; BaFin*) about its intention to offer the foreign investment units in the Federal Republic of Germany. Should the investment company not comply with this notification obligation, the regulator can prohibit the public sale of the investment units in accordance with

---

52 *Sacarcelik*, Rechtsfragen islamischer Zertifikate (Sukuk), p. 78 et seq.

Sec. 140 *InvG*. Furthermore, foreign investment units would be subject to the requirement to provide a prospectus in accordance with Sec. 137 *InvG*.

2. Classification under the KAGB

Domestic Sukuk

On the basis of the incorporation of the Alternative Investment Fund Managers (AIFM) Directive 2011/61/EU into German law, the Investment Act (*InvG*) was replaced by a new set of rules comprised in the capital investment act (*Kapitalanlagengesetzbuch, KAGB*). Both, domestic as well foreign sukuks can qualify under the rules of the new *KAGB* as alternative investment funds (*AIF*) and can be subject to the new rules of the *KAGB*. In particular the fact that the definition of alternative investment funds is very broad might have the consequence that sukuks will be subject to these rules. According to Sec. 1 Subsec. 3 KAGB the term AIF comprises all investment undertakings which do not require authorisation pursuant to Article 5 of Directive 2009/65/EC (meaning they are no undertakings for collective investments in accordance with the Directive 2001 107 EC and the Directive 2001 108 EC which fulfil the requirements set out in the Directive 2009/65/EU).

The main difference between the previous set of rules under the *InvG* and the new set of rules under the *KAGB* is that under the previous regulation it was determined whether an instrument qualifies as an investment on the basis of a more formal approach whereas under the *KAGB* the regulator will look at the substance.

The *KAGB* will be applicable towards an investment undertaking in the sense of Sec. 1 Subsec. 1 *KAGB*. Investment undertaking in the sense of Sec. 1 Subsec. 1 *KAGB* would be any undertaking for collective investments which collects capital from a number of investors in order to invest it on the basis of a pre-agreed management strategy for the benefits of these investors. Further it must not be an operational company outside of the financial sector.

The term of investment undertaking has most recently been explained in more detail in a letter of the *BaFin*.[53] The term "undertaking" is not based on the existence of a certain legal form. Whether the respective legal form can be approved or not is not subject to the legal form. Further a common investment in the sense of Sec. 1 Subsec. 1 *KAGB* requires that the investors will all be subject to the chances and risks of the undertaking. This prerequisite is fulfilled if the investors will participate in any profit as well as in any loss of the assets in which the undertaking has invested.

This also applies if the profit and loss participation of the investors is contractually limited.[54] However, Sukuks are in general indirectly guaranteed. Only in structures which are not common whereby the asset is sold in a true sale or in *Mudarabah* structures the investors might participate in a loss. Further in certain *Ijarah Sukuk* structures a loss participation cannot be excluded. According to the *BaFin* letter in minimum payment undertaking[55] does not exclude that a loss participation is offered. If the value of a unit is less than the guaranteed amount on the cut-off date which is relevant for the guarantee the capital investment company is obliged to pay the difference out of own means into the investment undertaking. In such case the investor participates in profit and loss of the undertaking. The loss protection in form of the minimum payment guaranteed in the form described above is only an indirect protection which is not relevant for the legal qualification.[56]

As set out above an *Ijarah Sukuk* is structured in a way that once the sukuk is due for repayment the assets which are subject to the sukuk will be repurchased by the relevant originator on the basis of a pre-agreed purchase price which covers in general a nominal amount of the Sukuk certificates. As a consequence the investor has only the credit risk with respect to the originator rather than the credit risk with respect to the underlying

---

53 BaFin, Auslegungsschreiben zum Anwendungsbereich des KAGB und zum Begriff des „Investmentvermögens", Geschäftszeichen WA 41-Wp 2137-2013/0001.

54 BaFin, Auslegungsschreiben zum Anwendungsbereich des KAGB und zum Begriff des „Investmentvermögens", Geschäftszeichen WA 41-Wp 2137-2013/0001.

55 Minimum payment undertaking according to Sec. 20 Subsec. 2 Nr. 7 KAGB.

56 See also *Sacarcelik*, Rechtsfragen islamischer Zertifikate (Sukuk), p. 79.

assets. Is the originator as the party which is obliged to repurchase the assets subject to insolvency proceedings the trustee will sell the assets which are subject to the Sukuk for the benefit of the investors. Should the assets which form the basis for the Sukuk have lost value during the term of the Sukuk the relevant SPV can only pay the investors their *pro rata* part in the enforcement proceeds. In such cases investors will suffer a loss.

Further requirements to qualify as an investment undertaking in accordance with the *KAGB* is that the undertaking gets it capital from numerous investors. This requirement is deemed to be fulfilled on the basis of the AIFM report of the ESMA if the undertaking or a person or a third party for the account of the undertaking makes directly or indirectly efforts to get capital in order to invest the capital on the basis of a pre-agreed management strategy.[57] In order to qualify as numerous investors it is not relevant whether in fact various investors have participated in the undertaking. It is only relevant whether there is a theoretic possibility that numerous investors participate.

A pre-agreed investment strategy is formed if the investment criteria are clearly set out and the discretion of the capital investment company is subject to investment conditions or a similar set of rules. With respect to the strategy of a Sukuk it can be argued that there is a certain investment strategy. However, the strategy is very limited. Further, the criterion of an investment for the benefit of the investors is in general also fulfilled. Such criterion is only then not fulfilled if the relevant issuer has only an own interest rather than an interest of the investors.[58] According to Sec. 1 Subsec. 1 sentence 1 *KAGB* the undertaking must not be an operational undertaking outside of the financial sector. The typical activities of an SPV such as leasing and administration of real estate or other assets are in general no operative activities. According to question 4 of the question catalogue of the BaFin letter financial leasing as well as operative leasing are investment activity so that all requirements of Sec. 1 Subsec. 1 sentence 1

---

57 BaFin, Auslegungsschreiben zum Anwendungsbereich des KAGB und zum Begriff des „Investmentvermögens", Geschäftszeichen WA 41-Wp 2137-2013/0001; ESMA/2013/600, p. 32.

58 BaFin, Auslegungsschreiben zum Anwendungsbereich des KAGB und zum Begriff des „Investmentvermögens", Geschäftszeichen WA 41-Wp 2137-2013/0001.

KAGB are in general fulfilled. In summary, the question whether a Sukuk forms investment undertaking in the sense of the *KAGB* depends on the qualification of the loss risk of the investor. If it has an unconditional guaranteed repayment claim it would not have the risk of loss. If the contractual arrangement of the SPV with the originator has the effect of a guarantee, the risk of loss is still inherent so that the SPV can qualify as investment undertaking.

However, according to Sec. 2 Subsec. 1 no. 7 *KAGB* the *KAGB* is not applicable with respect to securitisation companies. Securitisation companies are defined in accordance with Sec. 1 Subsec. 19 no. 36 *KAGB* , Sec. 1 Subsec. 2 VO 24/2009 ECB.[59] If the SPV qualifies as a securitisation company the *KAGB* is not applicable.

V. Final Remark

The article shows the potential hybrid character of Sukuks: Depending on the actual structure a Sukuk could qualify as fund or even as a securitisation. In either case the set of rules would be substantially different. The European legislator should react to the increasing popularity of these instruments by regulating them in a set of rules which is appropriate to their nature.

---

59 „*securitisation special purpose entities*" means entities whose sole purpose is to carry on a securitisation or securitisations within the meaning of Article 1(2) of Regulation (EC) No 24/2009 of the European Central Bank of 19 December 2008 concerning statistics on the assets and liabilities of financial vehicle corporations engaged in securitisation transactions and other activities which are appropriate to accomplish that purpose.

Discussion report to the lecture of Thomas Prüm

*Elias Bischof**

Prof. Dr. Karl Kreuzer (Würzburg) asks whether there are insurance options against 'Shari'a Risk'. – *Dr. Prüm* explains that Islamic schools quite often take a different approach when assessing the Shari'a compliance to a specific *Sukuk*. There is no regulator or supervisory authority which confirms Shari'a conformity. The choice of the scholar therefore will play a crucial role. His (or their) decision will be published in the documentation. At the end of the day it is the investor who bears the risk that Shari'a compliance of a specific *Sukuk* will in hindsight be questioned by other scholars. Accordingly, there is no insurance.

Dr. Merkel (Baden-Baden) asks as to who should interfere with the requalification process. – According to *Dr. Prüm* it is the Shari'a board often comprising of three to twelve scholars preferably with a good reputation. There is no supervisory body. Nevertheless there is the attempt to unify.

Prof. Dr. Götz Schulze (Potsdam) and *Prof. Dr. Matthias Casper* (Münster) both wonder whether Shari'a conformity means compliance with what is written or in a wider sense with the substance, i.e. the spirit of the Shari'a. – *Dr. Prüm* acknowledges that this is a crucial question which cannot however be answered unequivocally. *Dr. Asutay* adds that there is huge debate on this issue. The personal opinion of *Dr. Asutay* is that the prevailing view, which tends to follow the theory of the written form, falls too short. The spirit of the Shari'a should also be taken into account.[1]

Osman Sacarcelik (Münster) asks whether it is easier to set-up the *Sukuk* by certificate or investment fund. – *Dr. Prüm* states that the Sachsen-Anhalt *Sukuk* was a note (Schuldverschreibung). He concedes that

---

*   lic.iur., LL.M. (Edinburgh); Rechtsanwalt and Mediator, bischoflaw, Basel; research assistant and doctoral candidate, University of Basel.
1   See e.g. *Malaysia in Arab-Malaysian Finance v Taman Ihsan Jaya Sdn Bhd* (2008) 5 M.L.J 631 (HC(Mal)).

most recently certain scholars say that a note is fungible and therefore not Shari'a compliant.

Islamic Finance

Habib Motani[*]

Content and Discussion report to the lecture of Habib Motani

Elias Bischof[**]

I. Content

Referring to the two previous talks and discussions, *Mr. Motani* first explains that the practical problems of different schools of Shari'a are minor. These problems are analogous to different legal systems: as soon as the specific parameters to be applied are known (i.e. the law applicable in the respective jurisdiction, or the point of view of a specific Islamic school, which do not fundamentally differ on core principles), these parameters can simply be applied to the transaction in question. If a Malaysian document for instance, is not accepted in the Gulf region, which according to *Mr. Motani* is often the case, a way has to be found to make the Malaysian document acceptable. *Mr. Motani* adds that Sheik Taqi Usmani considered about 80% of *Sukuks* as not being Shari'a compliant. *Murabaha* for instance is one of those techniques which are not approved. Although Sheik Taqi Usmani's statement could concern *Sukuks* amounting to the value of billions of USD, his statement had no immediate consequences on existing contractual relationships, as parties are bound to the contract even if a later opinion raises doubts regarding Shari'a conformity. Normally there is a

---

*   Partner, Clifford Chance, London
**   lic.iur., LL.M. (Edinburgh); Rechtsanwalt and Mediator, bischoflaw, Basel; research assistant and doctoral candidate, University of Basel.

representation in the agreement that the scholars' view might differ from the investor's point of view. It is important that the buyer assures himself that the investment is Shari'a compliant. In the speaker's understanding a *Sukuk* is not a debt but rather an ownership participation and it is therefore similar to an equity.

Mr. Motani illustrates the Islamic financing principles and techniques in the context of hedging. He stresses that hedging is accepted and even encouraged by the IBF as a prudent form of risk management, especially to guard against exchange rate movements. The key aspect of Islamic hedging is that the transactions must be real transactions involving actual transfer of ownership of *halal* assets and not be speculative. The *wa'ad* (promise or undertaking) is the key feature. It might take the form of a promise to purchase an asset from the other party at cost plus a fixed amount based on the *Euribor* rate.

Mr. Motani explains that the organisation *International Swaps and Derivatives Association* (ISDA) and the *International Islamic Financial Market* (IIFM) have been working very closely with scholars to issue standard documents which would comply with the Shari'a.

In connection with applicable law, Mr Motani refers to the *Shamil Bank Case[1]*, in which *murabaha* agreements contained the following governing law clause: *'Subject to the principles of the Glorious Shariah, this Agreement shall be governed by and construed in accordance with the laws of England.'* The question was whether the *murabaha* agreements to be enforceable had to comply with both English law and the Shari'a. The Court denied, arguing that there could not be two separate systems of law governing the contract. English law was applicable because inter alia the Rome Convention requires that the law chosen must be the law of a country and the reference to the 'Glorious Shari'a' is insufficient to identify specific black letter provisions of the Shari'a.[2]

---

1   *Shamil Bank of Bahrain v Beximco Pharmaceuticals Ltd* (2004) 4 ALL E.R. 1072 CA (Civ Div).

2   The Court decision contains further reasons which led to the same result.

II. Discussion

Prof. Dr. Martin Schmidt-Kessel (Bayreuth) queries why a contract is binding and why there is not a frustrational purpose if a transaction is not Shari'a compliant. – *Mr. Motani* reasons that the parties agreed to a transaction in this specific way and that there is no frustration if the transaction is not Shari'a compliant.

Prof. Dr. Karl Kreuzer (Würzburg) asks 'choice of law'-clauses are in practice which do not decide upon English law. – *Mr. Motani* refers to the *Shamil Bank Case*[3]. He explains that in Saudi Arabia, Iran and in the Sudan the Shari'a is part of the legal system. If the law of one of these three jurisdictions is applicable, e.g. according to a choice of law clause in a contract, then a Court will have to apply the Shari'a.

Prof. Dr. Schmidt-Kessel raises the question whether any problem arises when the cost of a future purchase in connection with a *wa'ad* is determined by reference to *Euribor*. – *Mr. Motani* concedes that there are indeed problems, but scholars still accept the *Euribor* being that there is no alternative benchmark. Scholars will however probably not be prepared to accept the lack of alternatives for ever.

Oliver Loeck (Frankfurt a.M.) wonders if there is not an undue speculative element involved, if the price of a transaction depends upon the future exchange rate. – *Mr. Motani* asserts that this is not necessarily the case. It depends on the representations in the specific contract.

---

3   *Shamil Bank of Bahrain v Beximco Pharmaceuticals Ltd* (2004) 4 ALL E.R. 1072 CA (Civ Div).

Sharia Boards and Sharia Compliance in the context of European Corporate Governance[*]

Matthias Casper[**]

I. Introduction

According to one of the Hadith, the prophet said: "Gold for gold, silver for silver, wheat for wheat, barley for barley, dates for dates, and salt for salt - like for like, and hand-to-hand. Whoever pays more or takes more has indulged in *ribâ*. The taker and the giver are alike [in guilt].[1]. Read in conjunction with the Koranic verse that Allah permits commerce but prohibits usury (*ribâ*) (Sura 2, vers 275), the prohibition of *ribâ* has been the subject of controversies for centuries. However, this paper does not aim to discuss the logic behind the prohibition of *ribâ*, because it remains a fact that to this day, millions of Muslims worldwide obey the prohibition of charging interest.[2] Therefore, they are looking for financial products that are Sharia-compliant. This means investment forms that are compatible with the principles of the divine law. In reaction to this, the so-called Islamic Banking has been growing at annual double-digit rates for about 40 years. Worldwide, an entire Islamic financial sector has developed, even in *diaspora* countries such as Great Britain.

The question that comes to mind is whether Islamic prohibition of interest applies in secular countries such as Great Britain. This question is, however, misleading. Even in conservative Islamic countries *Sharia* law is

---

[*] This article is based on a lecture given at a conference „The Influence of Islam on Banking and Finance" hosted by the Ernst von Caemmerer Foundation and the Commerzbank in Frankfurt in October 2012 and the presentation form has been maintained. References will therefore not be exhaustive.

[**] Professor of Law, University of Münster.

[1] Narrated in major Hadith collections. For references see e.g. *Lohlker*, Das islamische Recht im Wandel, Münster 1999, p. 30.

[2] For the discussion on *ribâ* see e.g. *Saeed*, Islamic Banking and interest, Leiden 1999, pp. 41.

not directly applicable law. Especially the areas of civil and commercial law are usually governed by public, i.e. 'state made', law, which usually does not prohibit interest. Islamic Banking is voluntary in all countries but Iran and Sudan. Therefore, Islamic Finance can be defined as follows: It encompasses all kinds of financial services that are conducted without breaching the rules of the *Sharia,* although the contract itself is subject to a secular (national) jurisdiction.[3] There are no known examples where Islamic religious law was chosen as the governing law of a contract.

Regarding the coexistence of secular and religious law in the context of Islamic Finance, one can distinguish three models:

(1) Exceptionally, a state will declare religious laws to be directly applicable (e.g. in Sudan or Iran) or to be – like in Pakistan – examination criteria for all statutes enacted by the state. (2) The second model can be found in many Arab Gulf States. The Kingdom of Bahrain, one of the most important financial hubs for Islamic Finance, stands *pars pro toto.* These countries are characterized by a dualism of conventional banks and Islamic banks. The regulatory law currently puts Islamic banks in a separate category, which is supposed to safeguard that so-called *Islamic full-service-banks* comply with the objectives and principles of Islamic law. For conventional banks that offer both Islamic and regular financial products (so-called *Islamic Windows*), this framework aims to ensure that at least the Islamic products are in compliance with the Sharia.

However, this task is not exercised by the regular supervisory authority or another governmental agency. Instead, this supervisory function is delegated to the financial institution itself. The financial institution is obliged to establish a *Sharia Supervisory Board* (also shortened as *Sharia Board*), which has the duty to supervise the bank and confirm that its products and operations are in compliance with the precepts of the Sharia.[4] Sharia Boards are composed of Islamic legal scholars (so-called Sharia scholars) versed in economic and financial matters. They are paid but not employed

---

3   *Casper*, in: Jansen/Oestmann, Gewohnheit. Gebot. Gesetz, Tübingen 2011, pp. 301, 305.

4   For example, according to the Central Bank of Bahrain Rulebook Vol. 2 Part A, HC 9.2.1 Islamic banks are required to "establish an independent Sharî'a Supervision Committee complying with AAOIFI's governance standards for Islamic Financial Institutions No. 1 and No. 2", available on http://cbb.gov.bh.

by the company. The establishment of Sharia Boards has thus become a statutory duty, making them an integral part of the Islamic Finance architecture today.

(3) The situation is again different in countries with a predominantly non-Muslim population, such as the Member States of the European Union.[5] These countries are not interested in whether an Islamic bank operates in a Sharia-compliant way or not. Islamic banks in these countries may establish Sharia Boards but there is no legal obligation to do so. If they do choose to offer Islamic financial products, however, they may find it necessary to provide proof to their investors that their business conduct or at least their financial products are Sharia-compliant – for marketing purposes and beyond. Metaphorically speaking, Sharia Boards have become a "transformational conduit" between the religious laws and the investor who has chosen to adhere to its principles, although there is no obligation for him to do so in a secular country. The prime example for this model is Great Britain with its five Islamic banks. Germany may follow as soon as Islamic banks have gained a foothold there. A decision of the German Federal Financial Supervisory Authority (BaFin) on the application of Kuveyt Türk to establish the first fully Sharia-compliant bank in Germany is expected soon. Until now, there has been little demand for Islamic Finance among German Muslims.

This short overview has shown that the Sharia Board and the Sharia Compliance Departments within the financial institutions play an important role. Therefore Problems with Sharia Boards and Sharia Compliance Departments in the context of Corporate Governance shall be discussed. In a first step, the functions of a SSB will be explained and the differences to a Sharia Compliance Department. After a short presentation of the rules set forth by the AAOIFI and the IFSB for good governance of a Sharia Board, the focus will be on the question whether these rules are compatible with a "European" understanding of good Corporate Governance of financial institutions. It is important to highlight that when 'European Corporate Governance' is mentioned in this paper, reference is not made to a European Corporate Governance Codex, a subject which has

---

5   For an overview of regulatory issues with regard to Islamic Finance in various EU countries, see *Khan, M. F. / Porzio, M.*, Islamic Bankig and Finance in the European Union, Cheltenham 2010.

been brought up in the recent Green Book on Corporate Governance from April 2011 and the Green Book on Corporate Governance for Financial Institutes from 2010. Instead, the term European Corporate Governance is used in the sense of the common understanding of Corporate Governance in most Member States of the European Union, especially in Germany or the UK.

In a last step, the paper concentrates on the integration of internal Sharia Compliance into the context of European Corporate Governance.

II. Definition and Function of Sharia Boards

1. Overview

It is self-evident that the large number of Sharia Boards worldwide makes a uniform understanding of Sharia-compliant banking transactions impossible. There are two non-governmental-organizations that mainly contribute to a standardization of Islamic Finance. Besides the *Accounting and Auditing Organization for Islamic Financial Institutions* (AAOIFI), domiciled in Bahrain, the *Islamic Financial Services Board* (IFSB)[6] domiciled in Malaysia plays an important role with Kuala Lumpur being the second largest center for Islamic Finance worldwide. Although none of these two big standard-setting organizations explicitly admits to be following one of the four Sunni schools of law[7], these schools play an important role in deciding whether a financial product is Sharia-compliant.[8]

These organizations have enacted a large number of standards, similar to the German Corporate Governance Codex, which Islamic banks may

---

6   The IFSB expresses its self-understanding on its homepage: „The Islamic Financial Services Board (IFSB) is an international standard-setting organization that promotes and enhances the soundness and stability of the Islamic financial services industry by issuing global prudential standards and guiding principles for the industry".

7   The schools of law which are named after their founders are the *Hanafi, Shafiʿi, Hanbali* and *Maliki* schools. For a detailed overview on the emergence and nature of these schools see e.g. *Hallaq*, An Introduction to Islamic Law, Cambridge 2009, pp. 31.

8   For more Details see *Casper*, Corporate Finance Law, 2012, 170, 172.

not be legally obliged to follow but which are usually complied with by the banks. Therefore, the standards are typical for soft-law. There is an exception, however, for some states from the aforementioned 'model 2'-category. The regulatory law in Malaysia and Bahrain refers to some of these standards and therefore requires Islamic banks to follow their principles.

These principles will be looked at later when discussing whether they are compatible with the European understanding of Corporate Governance.

2. Functions

The Sharia Boards most important function is that of certification. This refers to the function of supervising the conformity of financial products with the Sharia law (see above I.). Normally, there are three Sharia scholars on the board which then examines the financial product. The process is often not very transparent. After examination, the SSB issues a *Fatwa* (legal opinion), in which the board confirms or negates compliance with the Sharia. A *Fatwa* is not considered a source of Islamic law.[9] Depending on the authority of the respective legal scholar, it can, however, be binding for devout Muslims. A common example will be presented further below. Furthermore, the *Fatwas*, which are usually written in or at least translated into English, will often be published on the internet, thereby making them available to a wider public. However, the reasoning and arguments are usually not disclosed in the Fatwa. Consequently, Sharia Board requires further analysis.

The certification function is accompanied by a supervisory function, which is especially important for Islamic banks. This function is already discernible from the name: *Sharia Supervisory Board* (SSB). In the case of an Islamic bank, the board will monitor the entire business organization to ensure that it is in accordance with the principles of Islamic law. In this

---

9   For the institution of *fatwa* and its applicability see *Hallaq*, The Origins and Evolution of Islamic Law, Cambridge 2005, pp. 62, 88-89; *Rohe*, Das islamische Recht, 2009, pp. 74; *Krawietz*, Der Mufti und seine Fatwa, Die Welt des Orients 26 (1995), pp. 161-180.

context, the AAOIFI Sharia standards – and some of the Sharia related principles of the IFSB – play an important role. For example, an Islamic bank is not allowed to invest in companies with unlawful (under religious law) business objectives. This includes alcohol or pork manufacturers or the publishers of certain dirty magazines. Some Sharia scholars even prohibit investments in any kind of entertainment media[10] because, as they state, „there is always something indecent about it".

But it is not the task of the SSB to monitor the liquidity management or profitability of a business. This is the task of the regular Supervisory Board or the Board of Directors of the bank.

The third function of the Sharia Boards is usually called the advisory function. This term is correct insofar as the management often seeks the advice of the Sharia Board before introducing a new product to the market, developing a new financial product, establishing new funds or developing a new investment policy. To this extent, the Sharia Board indeed exercises a certain advisory function. Nevertheless, just as the regular Supervisory Board, the Sharia Board only meets two to four times a year. Therefore, it is de facto unavailable for ongoing consulting. The advisory function could also come into conflict with the board's certification and supervisory functions. For this reason, the IFSB in particular recommends the establishment of an internal Compliance Department in addition to the Sharia Board.[11] This department is then responsible for the day-to-day questions of compliance with religious principles. Sometimes banks will solely rely on internal consultants. But even though these consultants, often people with a background in finance, will usually be well versed in questions of Islamic law, there is still a great difference to the Sharia Board. The internal consultants are not legal scholars and therefore cannot issue a Fatwa. In practice, Sharia Boards and internal consultants coexist. When it comes to aspects of applicability of legal norms and the role of the "transformational conduit", however, the external Sharia Board is the

---

10 See e.g. Dow Jones Islamic Market Indexes Rulebook, p. 4, http://www.djindexes.com/mdsidx/downloads/rulebooks/Dow_Jones_Islamic_M arket_Indices_Rulebook.pdf (accessed 07 October 2012).

11 See IFSB, Guiding Principles on Shariah Governance Systems for Institutions offering Islamic Financial Services, December 2009, Introduction, margin number 5; See also AAOIFI's Governance Standards No. 3: "The Shari'a review function may be located in the Internal Audit function of the bank."

solely relevant institution. This is why it is important to analyze its compatibility with European Corporate Governance.

In order for Sharia Boards to fulfill the above mentioned functions, three models exist to integrate the sharia advisor into a financial institution.

(1) Theoretically, one could discuss the integration of sharia scholars into the Managing Board or the Board of Directors. But usually Sharia scholars would not be willing to take upon a full-time job for only one Islamic financial institution. Also, the institute itself will only be interested in receiving the occasional certification or advice from the scholar but not in having a scholar be a permanent board member. Although some sharia scholars also have a background in finance, they normally do not possess the necessary qualifications for board membership of a financial institution (so-called "fit-and-proper-test").[12]

(2) For this reason, it is quite common for the Sharia scholars to organize themselves in a separate board which then exists alongside the Board of Directors. According to the AAOIFI Governance Standard for Islamic Financial Institutions No. 1 (1997), the Sharia supervisory board should be an independent body of legal scholars specialized in fiqh al-mua'malat (Islamic commercial jurisprudence) (Governance Standard No. 1 sub. 2). Additionally, the principles state that "every Islamic financial institution shall have a Sharia supervisory board to be appointed by the shareholders in their annual general meeting upon the recommendation of the board of directors" (No. 1 sub. 2). And, "[t]he Sharia supervisory board shall consist of at least three members. The Sharia supervisory board may seek the service of consultants who have expertise in business, economics, law, accounting and/or others" (No. 1 sub. 7).

From a German point of view, an SSB can be qualified as an advisory council (*Beirat*), which is, however, unfamiliar to the German Stock Corporation Act (AktG). Due to sec. 23 subsec. 5 AktG, the majority in the German literature assumes that the establishment of an advisory council is prohibited as there is no room for another supervisory body beside the Su-

---

12   For more details see *Casper*, Festschrift für Klaus Hopt, 2010, pp. 457, 471 et seq.

pervisory Board (*Aufsichtsrat*).[13] But this discussion – to my understanding – does not apply to the Sharia Supervisory Board. If there is a clear separation between the responsibilities of both organizations, and if the board of directors is still responsible for all decisions regarding the bank, there is no reason to qualify an SSB as an advisory council (*Beirat*). These issues will be further analysed below.

(3) Apart from the external SSBs, there are often internal Sharia Advisors or whole departments called Sharia Compliance Departments as already mentioned above briefly. According to No. 3 of the AAOIFI Governance Standard (1999), there is a duty to establish an internal Sharia compliance system: "The internal Sharia review shall be carried out by an independent division/department or part of the internal audit department, depending on the size of an Islamic financial institution (IFI)" (Governance Standard No. 3 sub. 2). "The internal Sharia review is an integral part of the organs of governance of the IFI and operates under the policies established by the IFI." (No. 3 sub. 3). "The head of the internal Sharia review shall be responsible to the board of directors." (No. 3 sub. 7).

This sounds similar to regular Compliance Departments whose establishment is mandatory for all financial institutions in the EU (see Art. 13 MiFID). But the difference is the same as that between the SSB und the Supervisory Board (*Aufsichtsrat*). The Sharia Compliance Department is exclusively concerned with breaches of Islamic law. In contrast, the regular compliance department has to ensure compliance with all laws and regulations governing the financial institution.

III. SSBs in the Context of European Corporate Governance

In comparative Company Law, Corporate Governance is understood as the objective of ideal and efficient administration of good management and controlling. To this extent, the existence of a religious "guardian council" is a clear alien element. On the other hand, there is no need to throw in the towel when keeping in mind the following aspects. Firstly, a too extensive

---

13　*Mertens,* in: Kölner Kommentar zum AktG Vor § 76 Rn. 28; *Habersack,* in: Münchener Kommentar zum AktG § 95 Rn. 6; *Hoffmann-Becking,* in: Münchener Handbuch zum Gesellschaftsrecht, tome 3: AG, 3rd ed. 2007, § 29 Rn. 19a.

influence by the Sharia Board has to be avoided as the bank's Executive Board must bear the ultimate responsibility for corporate actions[14] and it must remain independent from the SSB.

Secondly – and more importantly – the Sharia Board must meet three requirements in order to fulfill its certification and supervisory function while at the same time complying with our requirements for good corporate governance: (1) the board's independence from the corporate management, (2) the members' expertise and (3) the avoidance of conflicts of interest due to being dependent on the Company or due to dual mandates.

1. Independence of the Board of Directors (or the Managing Board)

From the German legal perspective, the ultimate responsibility of the Executive Board is a basic principle of company law as well as of regulatory law.[15] Hence, the Sharia Board's decisions cannot be binding for the company. Even if its decisions may be factually binding, legally the ultimate decision has to be made by the Executive Board of the respective bank, which bears the sole responsibility for the company's business policy.

Casting a quick glance at the Arabic countries, a different image becomes apparent. The English translation of Art. 58(a) sentence 2 of the Jordanian Banking Code reads as follows: „The board shall comprise not less than three members and its opinion shall be binding on the Islamic bank". The AAOIFI Principles on Corporate Governance – which are binding for example in Bahrain – use a very similar phrasing.[16] A different approach can again be found in Great Britain. English regulatory law allows freedom of legal arrangement and does not prescribe the establishment of a Sharia Board. But the Financial Services Authority (FSA) demands proof from Islamic institutions that, if a Sharia Board is installed, it only exercises an advisory function and does not interfere with the management of the institution. In an explanatory paper it is stated as follows: „The key point from the FSA's perspective is that firms can successfully

---

14   For a more detailed analysis see *Casper*, Festschrift Hopt, 2010, pp. 457, 472; *Sorge*, ZBB 2011, 363, 365 f.

15   See for example *Sorge*, ZBB 2010, 363, 365 f. with further references.

16   AAOIFI, Governance Standard for Islamic Financial Institutions No. 1, sec. 2.

show that the role and responsibilities of their SSB are advisory and that it does not interfere with the management of the firm."[17] It then goes on to state that this principle has worked for the existing Islamic banks in Great Britain. This is the path that the German regulatory law should also follow as long as no specific regulations for Islamic financial institutions exist. It would ensure that the general principles of banking regulation are adhered to.

Even if there will be no specific rules in German regulatory law on Islamic financial institutions in the near future, an Islamic financial institution located in Germany needs to take precautionary measures to avoid that the decisions of the SSB become formally or factually binding. First of all, clear rules regarding the duties and responsibilities of the SSB are important. It should be clear that the SSB has no direct influence on the decisions of the Managing Board. If the SSB objects to specific financial products or work processes within the financial institution and regards them as non-sharia-compliant, it should highlight different ways to solve the problem so that the Managing Board can choose between different alternatives.[18] In this context, one could resort to the principles set forth by the German Federal Court of Justice as to when consulting by an auditor is still deemed acceptable within the boundaries of sec. 319 subsec. 3 no. 5 Commercial Code (HGB). According to the Federal Court of Justice, the auditor may present alternatives on how to proceed to the Managing Board but he may not make the ultimate decisions himself.

2. Independence of the SSB

From the German and the European perspective, it does not seem to be problematic that the two trendsetters in Islamic Finance, the AAOIFI and the IFSB, demand that Sharia Boards should be independent from the financial institution and should not be subject to instructions from the com-

---

17 FSA, Islamic Finance in the UK: Regulation and Challenges, November 2007, www.fsa.gov.uk/pubs/other/islamic_finance.pdf, p. 13.

18 For more Details see *Sorge*, ZBB 2010, 363, 367 f.

pany.[19] However, it has to be rejected that the Sharia Board should be committed to the common good at the same time. This would privilege Sharia-compliant investment products over their conventional counterparts.

Nevertheless, there are no legal obstacles hindering the Sharia Board from acting not only in the interest of the bank but also in that of the investor. It could be said that the investor's interest to receive a Sharia-compliant investment product is not merely an insignificant "sentimental value". Rather, private autonomy also means that one can choose financial products that are compliant with personal ideals and beliefs. The assumption that the Sharia Board also acts in accordance with the interest of the investor is consistent with the aforementioned view that the Sharia Board assumes the function of a "transformational conduit" between religious laws and the investor.

According to the principles of AAOIFI, the members of a Sharia Board should be elected by the general assembly (Governance Standard No. 1 sub. 3). From the angle of German Corporate Governance, this is acceptable but not necessary. Due to the qualification of the SSB as an advisory board that reports to the Managing Board or the Board of Directors, it would also be thinkable that the Board of Directors or the Managing Board elects the members of the SSB together with the Supervisory Board.

3. Qualification and Conflict of Interests

At first glance, the Sharia Board members' expertise seems to be a trivial requirement. The devil, however, is in the details. First of all, a member should not only have a sound understanding of Islamic law but should also have adequate knowledge in finance. The latter is easy to assess, as one could require a degree in economics or finance or corresponding work ex-

---

19   IFSB Principle 3.1. (ref. 11) margin number 40 ff.; margin number 29 stresses, however, the responsibility towards shareholder interests; see AAOIFI Standards (ref. 16) No. 1 sec. 2, No. 5, sec. 2-7 with more emphasis on the independence. See also *Abd Jabbar*, Company Lawyer 2009, 243, 244.

perience. In contrast, there is no standardized education for scholars of Islamic law (*Sharia scholars*).

Consequently, there is only a very small number of qualified scholars with a sufficient background in economics or finance.

With qualified scholars being in short supply, one can observe a strong concentration on certain individuals. According to a survey by funds@work, *Nizam Yaqubi*, one of the most popular scholars, is a member in 85 (!) Sharia Boards at the same time.[20] If the same people sit on the boards of different, competing companies, this obviously implies a risk of conflicting interests. Therefore, there are many reasons for new regulatory principles aimed at avoiding such an extensive accumulation of mandates. From the German perspective, one could refer to the rules for the Supervisory Board (sec. 100 subsec. 2 AktG) whereupon an individual is not allowed to hold more than 10 mandates in different Supervisory Boards. At the "Deutscher Juristentag" in September 2012 in Munich a plea was made to reduce this number to six.[21] Of course, the discussion regarding sec. 100 AktG is not of equal significance with regard to Sharia Boards as the work load of the members of an SSB is not as extensive. However, 85 mandates are not acceptable under any circumstances. More importantly, a clear rule is needed to avoid conflicts of interest. If a scholar within the SSB is only concerned with the certification of Islamic financial products or the business process of an Islamic financial institution, it is not necessary to ban a membership in the board of a competing Islamic financial institution. But if the advisory function of the SSB plays an important role, there should be rules of incompatibility for the membership in SSBs of institutes that are in direct competition. The advisory function should primarily be fulfilled by the internal Sharia Compliance Department or Officer and not – at least not primarily – by the external SSB.

---

20 See report by funds@work, The Small World of Islamic Finance – Shariah Scholars and Governance, 19 January 2011, http://www.funds-at-work.com/uploads/media/Sharia-Network_by_Funds_at_Work_AG.pdf_03.pdf.

21 Beschlüsse der wirtschaftsrechtlichen Abteilung des 69. DJT Nr. 18, available under www.djt.de.

IV. Internal Sharia Compliance Systems in the Context of European Corporate Governance

The discussion on regular Corporate Compliance and Corporate Governance is still in the early stages.[22] One main question is whether non-financial listed stock corporations have the duty to establish a Compliance Department to prevent breaches of law.[23] But this question is not important in our context, because all Islamic Financial Institutions located in the EU indubitably have such an obligation to establish a Compliance Department, as governed by Art. 13 MiFID or section 33 German Securities Exchange Act (WpHG). Although the law speaks of "compliance functions" this can be understood as a duty to provide for a specific Compliance Department that reports directly to the Managing Board.

The question must be whether the principles of the AAOIFI on internal compliance are compatible with our understanding of compliance systems and whether the Sharia compliance function can be integrated into an existing regular Compliance Department.

According to the AAOIFI Standards "the internal Sharia review shall be carried out by an independent division/department or part of the internal audit department, depending on the size of an Islamic financial institution (IFI). It shall be established within an IFI to examine and evaluate the extent of compliance with Islamic Sharia rules and principles, fatwas, guidelines, and instructions issued by the IFI's Sharia supervisory board" (No 3. sub 2 part 1)." The first question that arises in this context is that of the independence of the Sharia Compliance Department. This requirement is already well known in the context of Corporate Compliance for financial institutions. In section 33(1) cl. 2 no. 1 of the WpHG, three requirements for the Compliance Department (called "compliance function" in the WpHG) within an investment services companies are listed: independence, effectiveness and permanence. But ever since the Circular Note on Compliance (MaComp)[24] by the Federal Financial Supervisory Authority (BaFin) it

---

22 For an overview see e.g. *Casper,* in: du Plessis/Großfeld/Luttermann/Saenger/ Sandrock/Casper, German Corporate Governance in International and European Context, 2nd ed. 2011, pp. 359.
23 Denying *Casper* (supra note 22), pp. 363.
24 Circular 4/2010 (WA) – *Mindestanforderungen an die Compliance-Funktion und die weiteren Verhaltens-, Organisations- und Transparenzpflichten nach §§ 31 et*

has been accepted that the members of the Compliance Department are independent from everyone but the Management Managing Board, which is responsible for the whole enterprise including compliance to all legal duties and therefore also the Compliance Department. To put it metaphorically: The Chief Compliance Officer is not a Janus-faced body who is obliged to protect both the interests of the company and those of the public – or in our context those of Allah. In other words, the Compliance Department does not constitute a branch of the police department or the prosecutor within the company.

From this point of view, another rule within the AAOIFI Governance Standards may be problematical: "The primary objective of the internal Sharia review is to ensure that the management of an IFI discharges their responsibilities in relation to the implementation of the Shari'a rules and principles as determined by the IFI's SSB." (No. 3 sub 2 part 2). "They shall have direct and regular communications with all levels of management, SSB and external auditors, which shall enhance the organizational status of the internal Sharia reviewers." (No. 3 sub 7). But on the other hand the principles of the AAOIFI clarify that: "The head of the internal Shari'a review shall be responsible to the board of directors." (No. 3 sub 7). And later on it is pointed out: "The head of the internal Shari'a review shall discuss conclusions and recommendations with appropriate levels of management before issuing a final written report." (No. 3 sub 20). This report has to be written four times a year and is addressed to the SSB as well.

This confirms that, even according to the principles of the AAOIFI, the internal Sharia Compliance Department falls under the responsibility of the Board of Directors or the two boards in the two-tier system. Compliance is a management task and not a public matter. The Sharia Compliance Department cannot be an extended arm of the SSB. The internal department does not automatically report potential breaches of Islamic law directly to the SSB. If these basic principles are accepted, there is no reason why the Sharia Compliance Department could not be integrated into

seq WpHG für Wertpapierdienstleistungsunternehmen (MaComp) from 7 June 2010, available under
http://www.bafin.de/cln_179/nn_722758/SharedDocs/Veroeffentlichungen/DE/S
ervice/Rundschreiben/2010/rs_1004_wa_*MaComp*.html.

the regular Compliance Department. However, it would be helpful if guidelines for the Compliance Department clearly set out the differences between the actions required by breaches of public and religious law, because the consequences are quite different.

V. Sharia Compliance and Sharia Risk

In a last step, the so called "Sharia risk" shall be analyzed. In early 2008 a very controversial debate arose on the question whether the issuer of a Sukuk (also called Islamic Bond) was allowed to guarantee the return of the invested capital. The originators behind the Special Purpose Vehicles (or external guarantors such as banks) had previously relieved the investors from any risks regarding the invested money. It was promised to the investors that they would get their invested money back at the end of the transaction. This practice was eventually permitted by many Sharia Boards.

In spring 2008, Sheikh Mohammed Taqi Usmani, who is the chairman of the Sharia Board of AAOIFI, entered the discussion and issued a Fatwa (legal opinion) in which he rejected these Sukuk-constructions which were equity-like in theory but in fact had debt-like features. In his opinion, there were no "entrepreneurial risks" for the investor. This was regarded as a violation of the principle of profit and loss sharing. As a reaction, the AAOIFI quickly updated its standards and also prohibited such constructions. The sale of the respective Sukuks on the secondary market became difficult and as a result, their price made a deep plunge.

What is the legal implication of such a scenario? Or to put it more precisely: Is there prospectus liability if the Sharia-conformity of a product is not given, either from the very beginning or later during the life-cycle of the Sukuk?[25]

The constellation, in which the lack of Sharia-conformity was certain ex ante or at least clearly foreseeable at the time of issuing the Sukuk, is clear. Prospectus liability is triggered in this constellation.

---

25 See *Casper*, Festschrift für U. H. Schneider, 2011, pp. 229, 242 and *Casper*, Die Rechtswissenschaft 2011, 251, 267.

An interesting question to be addressed is whether the issuer could expressly exclude liability with a disclaimer.

Sukuk prospectuses usually contain a recommendation that investors and potential investors should obtain information independently and consult their own Sharia advisors or similar reliable sources with regard to the conformity of the product with Sharia principles. Then the following disclaimer is included: "There is ... a risk that the status of Sharia compliance may change over time. The Company assumes no liability with respect to such changes."

Is such a disclaimer lawful? Addressing this question again leads to the crucial question: Who should bear the risk regarding the correct interpretation of religious laws? On the basis of German prospectus law, it can be suggested that the investors have voluntarily submitted themselves to the religious law which needs to be interpreted and is characterized by a diversity of opinions. Furthermore, the investor often knows and accepts that the prospective profit yield of a Sharia-compliant product might be lower than the market standard. Consequently, it would not be appropriate to shift the Sharia-risk entirely to the bank, issuer or Investment Company. On the other hand, the bank, issuer or mutual fund of course gains a financial advantage from the assumption of the Sharia-compliance of a product. Therefore, it would not be convincing to exempt the bank, issuer or fund from any liability.

As it is often the case, the solution is to be found in the middle. An indemnification clause or disclaimer is acceptable if the classification as Sharia-compliant by the Sharia Board is a legitimate interpretation within the boundaries of Islamic law. Only if there is a clear breach of Islamic law, i.e. in extreme cases, should the bank or issuer be liable for the incorrect prospectus. However, it seems feasible that an indemnification clause for Islamic financial products, whose religious legitimacy is in dispute among the different schools of law, is only valid if this dispute is pointed out within the prospectus. For example, a prospectus for a certain Islamic financial product could state that the certification as Sharia-compliant by the Sharia Board is based on the views of the Shafi'i school of law but is not necessarily accepted by all Muslim communities.

VI. Conclusion and Summary

As shown above: Sharia Supervisory Boards and European Corporate Governance are not like fire and water. They can be brought in line if the following eight guiding principles are observed.

1. Islamic Finance is voluntary.
2. Islamic Finance is not synonymous with the implementation of religious law. Although an Islamic Financial contract may be constructed in the view of the Islamic Law,[26] the relevant contracts are governed by secular state-made laws but at the same time the financial products are compatible with religious principles. Sharia Boards serve as a "transformational conduit" between religious law and the investor who wishes to adhere to its principles.
3. This objective is achieved through certification by the Sharia Boards. While this is the Board's most important function, it also fulfills a supervisory and an advisory function.
4. Sharia Boards can be embedded into the European understanding of Corporate Governance. For that, the management of the Islamic financial institution has to remain independent. Formal binding decisions of the Sharia Board – like required by the AAOIFI in their Corporate Governance Principles – are not compatible with European Corporate Governance. Only the Board of Directors or the Managing Board is ultimately responsible for the financial institution. The independence of the Sharia Board from the Management on the other hand does not pose a problem with regard to European Corporate Governance.
5. The number of mandates a single Sharia Scholar may hold should be limited. However the goal is not to stipulate a specific number but rather to avoid conflicts of interests, especially if the respective Sharia Board also serves as an advisor to the management.
6. It is preferable if the advisory function is mostly fulfilled by an internal Sharia Compliance Department. The internal Sharia review may be integrated into the regular Compliance Department as long as the

---

26 This is a consequence of private autonomy, for more details see *Casper*, Die Rechtswissenschaft 2011, 251, 257 et. seq. – also on the applicability of the principle of frustration of contract (§ 313 German Civil Code).

management continues to hold the sole responsibility for the financial institution and the internal Sharia Chief Compliance Officer does not report directly to the Sharia Supervisory Board.

7. Since there is no uniform interpretation of the Sharia, there is a risk that the Sharia-conformity of a product will be contested (Sharia Risk). It is not appropriate if either the investor or the bank/issuer are required to bear the entire risk of non-compliance by themselves.

8. Prospectus liability is confined to extreme cases of obvious breaches of the Sharia principles. An indemnification clause or a disclaimer is acceptable if the classification by the Sharia Board is a legitimate interpretation within the commonly accepted boundaries of Islamic law.

Discussion report to the lecture of Matthias Casper

Elias Bischof

Dr. Helmut Merkel (Baden-Baden) submits that under German law the supervisory board can form as many committees as it thinks necessary. The
Shari'a board might be seen to be such a committee. *Prof. Dr. Matthias
Casper* (Münster) points out several reasons why scholars might often be
unwilling to become members of supervisory boards, e.g. work load, responsibility, lack of expertise. The skills of the scholars often focus on religion and not on business issues.

Prof. Dr. Götz Schulze (Potsdam) disagrees with *Prof. Dr. Casper's*
second conclusion. In *Prof. Dr. Schulze's* opinion the general terms of the
contract for instance have to be construed in the light of the Shari'a. –
Prof. Dr. Casper agrees, but points out that it is the customer's choice to
decide the characteristics of the products (i.e. Shari'a compliance) he
wishes to purchase.

Finally *Prof. Dr. Martin Schmidt-Kessel* (Bayreuth) asks for clarifica-
tion regarding the impacts on Shari'a Supervisory Boards if, in hindsight,
a product is not considered Shari'a compliant. – *Prof. Dr. Casper* clarifies
that the board of directors would be responsible and liable if it confirms
that a specific product is Shari'a compliant although the SSB may say that
it is not. The SSB or its members might respectively be held liable if they
are considered to be shadow directors.

---

* lic.iur., LL.M. (Edinburgh); Rechtsanwalt and Mediator, bischoflaw, Basel; research assistant and doctoral candidate, University of Basel.

Towards a Global Contract Law in Banking and Finance? Inventory and Perspectives

Herbert Kronke[*]

I. Introduction

Grateful and honoured as I am for the invitation to participate in a high-level seminar organised by the foundation that bears the name of one of Germany's most brilliant and influential private law scholars, it is with some trepidation that I address this distinguished audience. This contribution is anything but a scholarly in-depth analysis of any of the specific areas where work has been done or is being done in the international arena. Rather, it is a modest inventory – a report.

A first note of caution needs to be stricken in relation to the very idea that there is, in the foreseeable future, a realistic perspective for contract law that is, firstly, global and that encompasses, secondly, the vast and diversified areas of banking and financial services. International organisations, governments involved in their work, professional and trade associations alike – we have all learned a few lessons from the past: the grand design of projects for the harmonised modernisation of commercial law, while sometimes firing academic imagination, is usually a recipe for failure. Conversely, conceptual modesty has borne fruit in a growing number of areas. Modesty may, for example, be reflected in the choice of a lower-key type of instrument, such as a model law, general principles, or other type of soft-law instrument rather than going for a binding treaty. Modesty may also lead governments and their formulating agencies to narrowly circumscribing the scope of an instrument – a minimalist approach geared at formulating unifying or harmonising rules only to the extent that is ab-

---

[*] Professor of Law and Director, Institute for Comparative Law, Conflict of Laws and International Business Law (University of Heidelberg) (on leave); Arbitrator, Iran-United States Claims Tribunal, The Hague (The Netherlands). Former Secretary General, UNIDROIT, Rome (Italy).

solutely necessary to achieve, for example, the objective of legal certainty of a given transaction.

On the other hand, the time has come to look beyond the boundaries of contract law. In light of the significant success of recent instruments dealing with property law and insolvency law, certainly no-go areas until 20 years ago, we may now cast the net wider and look at transactional law generally.

II. Organisations involved, their achievements, and projects

1. Organisations[1]

Among intergovernmental organisations, the global private-law formulating agencies Hague Conference on Private International Law, UNIDROIT and UNCITRAL are the most visible actors. However, regional organisations, such as the Organization of American States (OAS) and its special Conferences on Private International Law (CIDIP) or the *Organisation pour l'Harmonisation en Afrique du droit des Affaires* (OHADA) [2] have made valuable contributions to transnational banking and finance law. The European Union is not only a unique supra-national organisation but enjoys a type of genuine legislative power that has brought about the vast amount of instruments that shape today's banking and financial services in this part of the world; we may safely leave them aside to the extent that they are regulatory in nature[3].

---

1   For an overview of relevant organisations, their structure, and their working methods, see *Goode/Kronke/McKendrick,* Transnational Commercial Law. Text, Cases, and Materials (Oxford 2007) chapters 5 and 6.

2   See *Kwawo Lucien Johnson,* L'OHADA et la modernisation du droit des affaires en Afrique, Unif. L. Rev./Rev. dr. unif. 8 (2003) 71.

3   On instruments of transactional law, i.e. the Settlement Finality Directive (Directive 98/26/EC) and the Collateral Directive (Directive 2002/47/EC), see *Goode/Kronke/McKendrick* (n. 1) 13.28-13.33. The Directive 2009/44/EC of 6 May 2009 amending Directive 98/26/EC and Directive 2002/47/EC is reproduced, with introductory commentary, in *Goode/Kronke/McKendrick/Wool,* Transnational Commercial Law. International Instruments and Commentary, 2nd ed., Oxford 2012), 685 et seq., 723 et seq.

Another player of utmost importance is the European Bank for Reconstruction and Development (EBRD) whose 1994 Model Law on Secured Transactions shaped legislative developments in this area in particular in Eastern and Central European countries after the coming down of the iron curtain. While the World Bank as the foremost global economic development agency does not as such engage in commercial law reform, its sister organisation, the International Finance Corporation (IFC), does – in prominent cases in co-operation with specialists, such as UNIDROIT.

Among the non-governmental international organisations, the International Chamber of Commerce (ICC) and its specialised commissions is a long-time and reliable source of expertise. More recently, the International Swaps and Derivatives Association (ISDA), so far a successful promoter of benchmark industry know-how, has also provided valuable input for the development of instruments in intergovernmental negotiations.

Finally, regulators and their co-ordinating bodies have been seen as key participants in negotiations for the creation of transactional law. Suffice it to praise the pro-active and productive role played by the Bank for International Settlements (BIS) and, albeit with a different brief and perspective, central banks, including the European Central Bank (ECB).

2. Achievements[4]

Given the conservative environment of commercial finance it is by no means surprising that historically a non-governmental organisation took the lead. To a very large degree, the law governing international bank payment obligations is governed by uniform rules of banking practice published by the International Chamber of Commerce (ICC) and given effect by contractual incorporation into all relevant contracts entered into by banks with their customers and with beneficiaries of payment undertakings. The four sets of rules are: (i) the Uniform Customs and Practice for Documentary Credits (first published in 1933), known in the industry (in the version of the 2007 revision) as UCP 600 and used by banks all over

---

4   For all mentioned instruments, relevant texts, including status reports, and preparatory work, see the websites of the sponsoring organisations. For commentary, see *Goode/Kronke/McKendrick* (n. 1) and (n. 2).

the world; (ii) the supplement to their predecessor, UCP 500, covering electronic presentation, eUCP; (iii) the Uniform Rules for Demand Guarantees (first published in 1992), now in their revised version of 2010, URDG 758; (iv) and the International Standby Practices (ISP98), published in 1998.

To these must be added the 1995 UN Convention on Stand-By Letters of Credit and Independent Guarantees which moves the spotlights to UNCITRAL, which contributed two other instruments to the subject-matter area of this report: first, the 2001 UN Convention on the Assignment of Receivables, an as yet not very successful treaty, and the interesting and innovative UNCITRAL Legislative Guide on Secured Transactions.

It should be borne in mind that the ICC as the most trusted and successful organisation in the field is not a law-making body, and its rules are designed to produce consistency in banking practice. They therefore embody not only firm directions, which when incorporated into contracts give rise to legal rights and obligations in the same way as any other contractual provisions, but also certain exhortations as to good practice which banks are urged but not legally bound to follow. From the perspective of general commercial-law doctrine it is important to note, firstly, that contracting parties, courts, and arbitral tribunals widely take these instruments into consideration even in cases where a choice-of-law clause indicates the law of a certain state as the law governing the documentary credit or guarantee. And that would appear to be, secondly, the reason and legitimation why these bodies of rules – along with the INCOTERMS in the area of international sales – laid the foundations of the contemporary discussion of concepts such as (new) lex mercatoria, soft law, and the like.

Among the intergovernmental organisations UNIDROIT is certainly the most experienced and productive one. Its expertise was incrementally built over a period of almost three decades and following conceptual logic, industry-inclusive processes as well as a keen awareness of priorities, albeit restrained by scarcity of resources.

The point of departure was Ottawa where, in 1988, the UNIDROIT Conventions on International Factoring and on International Financial Leasing were adopted. While the former had limited apparent success (although it contributed significantly to the understanding and the development of the law of assignment in a number of jurisdictions), the latter not only provided a basis addressing the conceptual problems of the three-partite situation (removal of responsibility from the lessor to the supplier, liability to third parties, protection against the lessee's insolvency, and default remedies of the lessor), the convention was also instrumental in setting financial leasing free from its unfortunate identification with traditional hire or hire-purchase contracts and recognising its character as a secured-financing transaction. Twenty years later, in 2008, a Model Law on Leasing developed and now promoted in co-operation with the IFC and catering, in particular, for the needs of developing countries was adopted[5].

Asset-based secured financing entered a new era when, in 2011, the Cape Town Convention on International Interests in Mobile Equipment and the first (of three) industry-specific protocols, the Protocol on Matters Specific to Aircraft Equipment, were adopted. Among its key features there is firstly, the recognition that, functionally, a finance lease, a classic security agreement and the reservation of title in a sale, are close relatives and that they should be treated as equals: the Cape Town Convention created, therefore, the umbrella concept of the "international interest" which encompasses all three types of collateral arrangement. Secondly, the Convention and the protocols provide for default remedies and clear priorities, including in cases of insolvency of the collateral provider. Thirdly, an international registry – notice based and fully automated – provides the necessary infrastructure for the protection of priorities in particular in the debtor's insolvency. The success is overwhelming: 57 States and the European Union are parties to the Convention and the Aircraft Protocol, and it is said that between 75 and 80 % of all secured transactions for the acquisition of aircraft worldwide are covered by the instruments. A second protocol – on matters specific to railway rolling stock – was adopted in 2007 in Luxembourg and a third one, extending the potential benefits to the secured financing of space objects (telecommunication satellites, meteorological satellites, etc.) was adopted in 2012 in Berlin.

---

5   On both the Ottawa Convention and the Model Law (as well as the Cape Town Convention as an instrument covering financial leasing) and their implementation in various jurisdictions, see national reports from Belgium, Canada, China, Croatia, France, Greece, Italy, the Netherlands, Poland, Turkey, the United States aw well as from the OAS and UNCITRAL and a comparative General Report by *Kronke,* Financial Leasing and its Unification by UNIDROIT, Unif. L. Rev. 16 (2011) 23-504.

The 2009 Geneva Convention on Substantive Rules for Intermediated Securities[6] was a response to the fundamental changes which the global securities markets and the systems for clearing, settlement and custody had undergone since the dematerialisation of securities had set in, beginning in the 1970s[7]. Some jurisdictions had developed internally working mechanisms which, however, were not internationally compatible. The majority of legal systems had previously no functional rules that addressed the multi-layer intermediated holding patterns for dematerialised financial instruments at all. What is in light of the title of this contribution important to note, however, is that both the 2009 UNIDROIT Geneva Convention and its conflict-of-laws companion, the 2006 Hague Convention on the Law Applicable to Certain Rights in Respect of Securities held with an Intermediary[8], are essentially instruments on property law – i.e. title to securities, their acquisition and disposition, the use of financial instruments as collateral, protection in cases of insolvency, etc. In other words and as already noted, transnational commercial law has transcended the boundaries of contract law.

---

6   See, in particular, *Kanda/Mooney/Béraud/Thévenoz/Keijser,* Official Commentary on the UNIDROIT Convention on Substantive Rules for Intermediated Securities (Oxford 2012). The most comprehensive source on the subject will be *Thomas Keijser* (ed.), Transnational Securities Law (Oxford, forthcoming). On the relationship between the (Geneva and Hague) Convention(s) and domestic law and implementation in Swiss law, see *Kuhn/Graham-Siegenthaler/Thévenoz* (ed.), The Federal Intermediated Securities Act (FISA) and the Hague Securities Convention (HSC) (Berne 2010); *Zobl/Hess/Schott* (eds.), Kommentar zum Bucheffektengesetz (BEG) (Zürich 2013). On the need for and prospective implementation of the Convention in German law *Kronke,* Das Genfer UNIDROIT-Übereinkommen über materiellrechtliche Normen für intermediär-verwahrte Wertpapiere und die Reform des deutschen Depotrechts, Wertpapier-Mitteilungen 2010, 1625.
7   For an overview, see *Gullifer/Payne (*eds.), Intermediated Securities (Oxford, Portland/Ore. 2010).
8   See, in particular, *Goode/Kanda/Kreuzer/Bernasconi,* Hague Securities Convention. Explanatory Report (The Hague 2005). For a German perspective, see *Einsele,* Das Haager Übereinkommen über das auf bestimmte Rechte im Zusammenhang mit zwischenverwahrten Wertpapieren anwendbare Recht, Wertpapier-Mitteilungen 2003, 2349; *Reuschle,* Grenzüberschreitender Effektengiroverkehr, RabelsZ 68 (2004) 687.

So far, this report made reference to international instruments aimed at harmonised modernisation specifically of areas of banking and finance law. It must not be overlooked, however, that the organisation in charge of these endeavours in parallel produced an instrument dealing with the law of contractual obligations, the UNIDROIT Principles of International Commercial Contracts, a widely acclaimed soft-law instrument which, in its third edition (of 2010), now provides an almost complete "general part" of contractual obligations, and which is not only increasingly used in the practice of drafting contracts as well as in international commercial arbitration but which also served as a model and source of inspiration for contract law reform from the Netherlands to China, from Germany to Japan, from Estonia and Lithuania to Argentina, Mexico and the Russian Federation.

3. Work in progress

The 2009 Convention on Intermediated Securities contains a few provisions regarding netting specifically in that context (Articles 31 to 38). At the request of the financial industry, in particular ISDA, UNIDROIT immediately after the Convention's adoption began work on a draft convention on netting of financial instruments. The rationale behind the project was to do more for a robust legal infrastructure than ISDA's master agreements were capable of achieving in emerging markets. A treaty, i.e. "hard law", was considered to be the functionally appropriate approach – as generally in matters where the law touches upon the rights of more than the two parties to a contract. However, as the work proceeded, some members of the Study Group and the UNIDROIT Governing Council first and then also governments participating in the Committee of governmental experts, arguably under the impact of the European financial crisis, seem to have become more cautions – or less courageous –, and the project is now on its way to completion in the form of a soft-law instruments, the Principles on the Operation of Close-out Netting Provisions.

Another project which, in 2003, had been put on the UNIDROIT work programme with a view to counter-balancing the work on intermediated securities (considered to be of interest primarily for sophisticated jurisdictions and highly developed markets), is a future Legislative Guide on Principles and Rules Capable of Enhancing the Trading in Securities on

Emerging Markets. At this point in time, it would appear to have been merged into the work of a special Committee established in 2008 at the diplomatic Conference for the adoption of the Convention on Intermediated Securities, the Committee on emerging markets issues, follow-up and implementation of the Convention. In other words, the minimalist approach chosen by the drafters of the Convention, i.e. their decision to address only key issues where uniform substantive law was essential to ensure internal soundness and cross-border compatibility[9], inevitably left vast blanks and entailed no fewer than twenty-nine references to the "non-convention law" (Article 1 (m)). While this makes obvious sense in a domestic legal system that has statutory or judge-made law covering those areas, a country which does not – and that is the majority of countries – needs to catch up with those where banking and securities law has been constantly developed over decades and in some cases centuries. A legislative guide for the implementation of the Convention ("implementation kit") will in many of those jurisdictions eventually turn out to be a legislative guide (if not a code) for securities-related financial services law.

III. Involvement of States with Islamic legal systems

It is assumed that for the purposes of this symposium it is of interest to which extent relevant instruments were developed (and hard-law instruments negotiated) with active participation of States whose legal system is based on Islamic principles. The yardstick may be the widely discussed fact that the 1980 UN Convention on the International Sale of Goods (CISG) was negotiated with relatively little participation from such countries, and that certain key provisions were not included in the eventually adopted text due to their resistance. A second remark would appear to be in order, and that is that two very important countries with a majority muslim population, Indonesia and Turkey, in light of the distinctly secular traits of core elements of their private and commercial law cannot be included in that group. And yet, given their current governments' inclination

---

9   See The UNIDROIT Study Group on Harmonised Substantive Rules Regarding Indirectly Held Securities, Position Paper August 2003, UNIDROIT 2003, Study LXXVIII Doc. 8, 15 et seq.

to at least promote Islamic values in public life, their participation will be mentioned where appropriate.

The 1988 Ottawa Conventions on Financial Leasing and on Factoring were negotiated with Algeria, Egypt, Guinea, Malaysia, Morocco, Senegal, Sudan (and Turkey) actively participating.

The 2001 Cape Town Convention on International Interests in Mobile Equipment and the Aircraft Protocol were negotiated with no fewer than nine Islamic States (plus Turkey) participating: Bahrain, Egypt, Iran, Jordan, Libya, Oman, Pakistan, Sudan, and the United Arab Emirates. Although Malaysia and Syria had not participated, both countries ratified the two instruments relatively early. In the meantime, Indonesia too ratified.

Algeria, Indonesia, Jordan, Libya, Tunisia and Qatar were all proactively involved in the finalisation of the 2007 Luxembourg Rail Protocol.

The 2012 Berlin Space Protocol to the Cape Town Convention saw Iran, Iraq, Pakistan, Saudi Arabia, Senegal, Sudan and Yemen (plus Turkey) as participants in the negotiations.

Egypt, Indonesia, Jordan, Malaysia, and Morocco were involved in the negotiations leading to the adoption of the 2006 Hague Securities Convention. It deserves special mention that the Malaysian delegation was probably the most active one if one excludes the North Americans, the West Europeans, Australia and Japan.

Indonesia, Iran, Kuwait, Oman, Pakistan, Qatar and Sudan (plus Turkey) were involved in the negotiation of the 2008 Model Law on Leasing. Oman hosted – a *première* in the history of transnational commercial law – one session of the Committee of governmental experts, and it is said that Oman and the Palestinian Authority will be the first ones to implement the Model Law.

The 2009 Geneva Intermediated Securities Convention was negotiated with participation from Bangladesh, Egypt, Indonesia, Libya, Morocco, Qatar, Saudi Arabia, Senegal (and Turkey).

As regards work in progress specifically related to financial markets law, the Committee on emerging markets issues, follow-up and implementation (which is an open as well as an open-ended committee co-chaired by Brazil and China) has so far held two working sessions in which Pakistan and Saudi Arabia participated.

Iran, Saudi Arabia (and Turkey) are involved in the work of the Committee of governmental experts in charge of preparing draft Principles on the Operation of Close-out Netting Provisions, a project that is expected to be finalised and a text to be adopted in 2013.

Finally, experts from Egypt, Iran and the United Arab Emirates served on one of the Study Groups for the preparation of the UNIDROIT Principles of International Commercial Contracts (1994, 2004, 2010).

IV. Principal challenges

1. Transactional law and regulatory law

From a conceptual point of view there is a straight forward distinction between transactional law on the one hand and regulatory law on the other hand. In particular in the areas of trading in securities, banking and financial-services law the distinction has always been there. And member States' governments have always had a strict approach in seeing to it that the private-law formulating organisations did not overstep the borderline. This is true both for the formulation of work programmes, i.e. the assignment of specific projects to, for example, the Hague Conference or UNIDROIT, and the conduct of inter-governmental negotiations. Until the start of the negotiations which brought about the Hague Securities Convention or, more precisely, almost until the end of that process and the adoption of the draft Convention, no one had ever suggested that that instrument was heading for problems flowing from its perceived venturing into the realm of regulatory law. When a consensus on the primary rule, Article 4, i.e. the principle of party autonomy for the determination of the governing law, emerged and the question was raised as to how far that would reach, the provision on the scope of the Convention and of the applicable law (Article 2(1) and (2)) as well as the limits of its scope (Article 2(3)) were considered to be sufficient to ensure that the instrument would not encroach upon the State parties' continuing and full autonomy to determine their regulatory framework for intermediated securities. Only when the Convention had been adopted did fierce lobbying (it is said by one very powerful financial institution and the government of its home country) set in alleging that regulatory law, indeed, was about to be unhinged in the interest of financial institutions of certain other countries. Since then, the Hague Convention, is considered to be in protracted coma, if not deceased.

To prevent similar political games from being successful in torpedoing the future adoption of the 2009 Geneva Convention on Substantive Law on Intermediated Securities, at the second session of the diplomatic Conference the draft Preamble was amended, and the last two recitals on Contracting States' uninfringed power to regulate and oversee transactions were added. To no avail, as it appears today. The EU Commission – or certain governments' unchallenged power in Brussels – played a particularly unpleasant role in both instances.

2. Regionalism and global initiatives

The harmonization of private and, in particular, commercial law has always had to take the relevance of regions into account[10]. Indeed, some commentators have described the universal harmonization of private law in the late nineteenth and the first half of the twentieth centuries as "regional harmonization in disguise"[11]. While the Latin American countries and Japan were involved, at least in work carried out at UNIDROIT, from as early as the 1920s there can be no doubt that the agenda of institutional harmonization at a worldwide level was largely driven by a regional, to wit European, political and academic discourse. Today, however, we are not back at square one. On the contrary, the member States of the EU have transferred sovereign powers – not least in the area of securities and financial markets as well as private international law, but also, albeit to a varying and lesser extent, limited areas of private and even insolvency law – to the Union. The pieces of this mosaïque will, hopefully, sooner or later fall into place. For the time being, the constitutionalization process in Europe entails, however, massive problems for any global initiative. They are manifold. First, initially neither the Commission nor the member States' governments knew exactly who had which competences and how to coordinate them internally and vis-à-vis the non-Europeans; this problem af-

---

10 See the vast number of contributions in: Worldwide Harmonisation of Private Law and Regional Economic Integration, Acts of the Congress to Celebrate the 75th Anniversary of the Founding of the International Institute for the Unification of Private Law (UNIDROIT), Unif. L. Rev./Rev. dr. unif. 8 (2003) 1-593.

11 *Basedow,* Worldwide Harmonisation of Private Law and Regional Economic Integration – General Report, Unif. L. Rev./Rev. dr. unif. 8 (2003) 31.

fected the Cape Town (and to a greater extent the Hague) negotiations until the EU ratified the Cape Town Convention and the Aircraft Protocol (and until the EC/EU acceded to the Hague Conference). Secondly, the Commission has so far not ensured that (available and first-rate!) resources are employed in the global processes in a sustained manner. Thirdly, the Commission – be it unconsciously, be it willingly, be it of its own doing, be it at the behest of one or more member States' government(s) – is frequently not acting and arguing honestly and in a transparent manner; the Geneva Convention is, unfortunately, a telling example[12]. Fourth, the European Union has its own – much more detailed and much denser – political agenda, as has become ever more obvious during the financial crisis since 2008. The need for an own agenda – mismanaged as it may at certain points in time have been by member governments, the Commission, and the ECB – is undeniable and it presents problems for the non-Europeans and, importantly, for all projects and processes at the global level.

At the same time, we have seen first signs of inter-regionalism focused on substance. For example, the MERCOSUR (the South American Common Market) and SADC (the Southern African Development Community) participated, as observers, at the Luxembourg diplomatic Conference for the adoption of the Rail Protocol to the Cape Town Convention.

For the time being, there are no signs to suggest that any of the intergovernmental organisations of the Islamic States could develop activities in the area of the law of commerce and finance. While organisations such as OHADA may have regard to the situation of any predominantly Muslim member State and while others among whose member States there are also Islamic States, such as Malaysia and Indonesia in the framework of ASEAN, may from time to time announce that an option of extending their activities to economic law is being explored, it is unlikely that initiatives touching upon transactional law in the area of banking and finance will be launched in those quarters any time soon.

---

12 For current evaluation, see *Keijser* (n. 6); *Estrella-Faria,* Harmonisation of Securities Law at the Global and European Level: Implications for Company Law, Ministry of Justice of the Republic of Latvia, Company Law Conference 2012, Riga, 20-21 September 2012.

3. Diversity of stakes and strategies

Any reflection on the perspectives of global contract – or transactional – law on banking and financial services will need to start based on the acknowledgement that there has never been – and arguably will never be – a coincidence, or harmony, of stakes that individual States or groups of States have in either the process or the outcome of any of the projects, past, present, or future. Moreover, even where the stakes coincide the strategies employed vary widely or are even opposed, and this is true not only for any given point in time but may change over time. In the abstract, one might say that there are pro-active governments who take a stance and invest resources in any of the initiatives either because their domestic stakeholders (industry, the legal profession) lobby them to do so or because they are disinterested benefactors who want to make the world a better place.

Conversely, there are the innocent by-standers – or sitters on the fence – who may be either historically committed to participating in academic discussions or intergovernmental negotiations or refrain from any involvement due to (real or purported) lack of resources. Lastly, there are countries where neither governments nor the academic or professional communities have the interest and/or the know how necessary for meaningful participation.

The following examples may explain that kind of characterization. The Cape Town Convention on International Interests in Mobile Equipment and the Protocol on Matters Specific to Aircraft Equipment enjoyed, obviously, top priority and full governmental and parliamentary support (a) in countries where leading manufacturers of commercial aircraft or aircraft engines are located; (b) in countries where financial institutions (banks and lessors) involved in aviation finance are located; (c) in countries where potential buyers/lessees/borrowers-security providers, i.e. airlines interested in asset-based financing of acquiring commercial aircraft, are located; (d) where either the status quo of secured-transaction law or its reform are a matter of political – or at least scholarly – concern. In relation to the above-mentioned hypothesis of governments changing views over time, (e.g.) European airlines whose financial situation was excellent and who, in 1999, paid equipment in cash and were, therefore, not interested in improving borrowing conditions for competitors in countries with a less robust legal infrastructure, were quick to change their – as well as their respective governments' – analysis when either their own financial situation deteriorated or when they acquired a stake in a carrier based, for example, in Africa or Latin America. Both the intensity and the direction of participation of any national – e.g., German, US, Luxembourg – banking community and, consequently, the respective government – in relation to either the Rail or the Space Protocol to the Cape Town Convention varied significantly under the impact of the afore-mentioned and other – mostly economic – incentives and disincentives.

In a similar vein and unsurprisingly, only very few governments of States with complete, time honoured and sophisticated securities law show active interest in advancing the work on a legislative guide for emerging markets (*supra* II 3).

At least for the time being, there are no indications of common stakes and common strategies of Islamic States as well as private-sector players in those States in respect of modernised harmonisation of commercial law, in particular banking law at the global level.

V. Conclusions

The question raised in the title of this paper was obviously meant to be provocative. Rather than answering in an equally provocative manner, i.e. with a crude "no", there are good reasons to give a more prudent answer. "Global" would appear to be a notion raising issues of measure, degree, and time horizons. The financial industry will in all likelihood continue to go forward, where appropriate, with soft-law instruments such as the UCP, the URDG, etc. The development banks, too, may choose to follow that route. Where necessary and appropriate, governments will increasingly look to the private-law formulating agencies as well as the central banks for advice and specific proposals in the form of draft hard law, i.e. conventions. To what extent "regional economic integration organisations" – still a neutral misnomer for the EU and no one else – or other regional organisations will be of assistance or, on the contrary, obstruct the global developments remains to be seen. While in 2005 the answer would have tended to be in the affirmative, more recent experiences may foster scepticism. The critical questions which call for answers on a case-by-case basis are whose agenda and whose priorities will be the driving forces tomorrow and in the long term.

Discussion report to the lecture of Herbert Kronke

Elias Bischof*

Prof. Dr. Felix Maultzsch (Frankfurt a.M.) asks whether the approach to unify is considered to be rather principle than rule based. – *Prof. Dr. Kronke* agrees that the Anglo American approach used to be rather principle based. Nevertheless the USA, the United Kingdom and Australia all played an important role in putting forward the initiative to harmonise the law of commerce on a world-wide level, especially with regard to the conflict of laws rules.

Prof. Dr. Karl Kreuzer (Würzburg) points out that in contrast to the negotiations of The Hague Securities Convention 2006, where a huge effort was necessary to correct the perception that it did not enact regulatory law but private law, the negotiations of the Geneva Securities Convention 2009 took a much more integrative approach from the very beginning. Without focussing on substantive legal rules they were thus, in his view, more successful. – *Prof. Dr. Kronke* agrees.

Prof. Dr. Kreuzer agrees that it is the ideal to ask and to listen to 'the industry', but then adds for consideration that such projects may fail too. He refers to the Space Protocol 2012. The initiative came from the industry itself but at a later stage has consequently been undermined by it. – *Prof. Dr. Kronke* specifies that one of the initiators of the Protocol was a small company which had grown larger and larger until it almost held a monopoly. It was then no longer in the interests of the company to have a global protocol which provided legal certainty to small companies.

Finally *Dr. Helmut Merkel* (Baden-Baden) and *Prof. Dr. Peter Jung* (Basel) ask as to what extent Islamic countries participate in the developments of harmonisation, what their stakes and strategies are and what impacts the most recent Arab revolutions may have. – *Prof. Dr. Kronke* emphasises that some countries have been absent from international negotia-

---

*   lic.iur., LL.M. (Edinburgh); Rechtsanwalt and Mediator, bischoflaw, Basel; research assistant and doctoral candidate, University of Basel.

tions for quite a long time and have only recently decided to participate more actively, e.g. Indonesia in 2007 and Saudi Arabia in 2008. Iran even volunteered to host one of the meetings, which is the first time that this geographic region has acted proactively. It remains to be seen what approach the new governments in the Arabic States will take. – *Prof. Dr. Kreuzer* adds that Islam states are becoming increasingly involved at an international level. Saudi Arabia for instance took a very active part in the negotiations of the Space Protocol 2012. – *Dr. Asutay* detects an increasing pragmatic approach on the part of Islamic countries.